TheRealGuide's Penang Complete Visitor Handbook is revised annually to be the most up-to-date guide to Malaysia's premium travel destination.

The original idea of a personal guidebook, with a handbook section to make it easy for visitors to plan for their stay in Penang, has grown to make this publication one that even those resident in Penang can use - to enjoy the state's many attractions, products and services.

This 2001 edition includes more information with many large-scale maps. It is also the third annual compilation of Penang's unique attractions which have made this island-hinterland state of Malaysia a true world travel destination.

Penang has been attracting travellers to its shores for over two hundred years now. Today, it is favoured by travellers with a yen for exploration and discovery, conference attendees with a taste for the exotic, and manufacturers who wish to locate their operations in a bit of paradise.

Perpustakaan Negara Malaysia Cataloguing-in-Publication Data
The Real Guide's Penang: Complete Visitor Handbook - 3rd Edition
    ISBN   983-40502-0-8
    1. Penang -- Description and Travel -- Handbooks, manuals, etc
    915.95113

3rd Edition 2001
Published by Coda Designs
2 Lorong Bunga Kaca Piring, Tanjung Bungah, 11200 Penang, Malaysia

© Coda Designs 2001

Printed in Penang

Acknowledgements

The publisher would like to thank the Penang Development Corporation (Tourism Division) for its support, past and present.

The publisher would also like to thank Ms Yeoh Lean Looi for her help in transcribing all printed text received into machine readable form for use in the production of this book.

Thanks also go to Sarah Tan for taking the many photographs required to ensure the currency of the publication and the complete preparation of the book's new layout, and, to Lee Kwong for his work on the publication's maps.

Finally, the publisher would like to offer much belated thanks and sincere apologies to Chuah Kok Heng and Neoh Choo Lim who did such a magnificent job in capturing the many images used in the 1999 Edition of *TheRealGuide's* PENANG Complete Visitor Handbook.

PREFACE

The small island-hinterland state of Penang in Malaysia is very much an amalgam of the old and the new.

Modern commercial towers rise from one of Southeast Asia's largest collections of prewar buildings. Manufacturers of sophisticated electronic goods compete for space with temples, mosques, and century-old churches. The latest fashions are worn by a people whose ways of life still mirror those of their forebearers.

For sheer variety of locales, cultures, and foods, Penang is hard to beat.

It has cool hill stations, warm stretches of fine sandy beaches, a historic city which is still largely unchanged from the settlement first laid out by its founder, Sir Francis Light, as well as traditional Malay *kampungs* (villages).

The descendants of Penang's original Malay, Achehnese, Arab, Batak, Bengali, Bugis, Boyanese, Burmese, Cantonese, Hainanese, Hakka, Hokkien, Malabari, Malayali, Mandaliling, Minang, Parsi, Pathan, Portuguese, Punjabi, Rawa, Siamese, Sindhi, Tamil, Teochew, Telugu and other peoples who have settled here may have become Penangites, but most continue to live as a distinct culture, holding on to their respective traditions and customs.

The seamless melding of the many peoples in Penang is best reflected in the foods they enjoy. With the foods of each race being influenced by the taste of another's, most Penang dishes are unique combinations of ingredient, sauce, garnishing and seasoning. Light's "all-comers" acceptance of settlers also resulted in Penang's concoctions in hawker foods, most of which are now touted throughout Malaysia.

For those who live here, Penang is a village township where people can, and do, talk to people, where most move without desperate speed, and modernity is a convenience to be savoured, experienced or discovered. For visitors, Penang is likely to be a place where time stood still.

Telephone : 60-4-2614424
Fax : 60-4-2613003

CHIEF MINISTER'S OFFICE
10502 KOMTAR
PENANG, MALAYSIA

Your Ref :
Our Ref :

MESSAGE FROM THE RIGHT HONOURABLE
CHIEF MINISTER OF PENANG

I am pleased to see the continuing improvements made in TheRealGuide's Penang Complete Visitor Handbook as reflected in this 2001 edition of the publication.

It is our intention to make the publication increasingly useful in its coverage of Penang's many attractions and services - to make it a book that both visitors and Penangites can refer to, for all that the state can offer them.

As in the past, all care will be taken to provide genuinely usable information for those who wish to visit Penang or make use of its, oftentimes, unique range of products and services.

I look forward to welcome you to the discovery and exploration of Penang - Malaysia's premier travel destination.

Thank you.

(TAN SRI DR. KOH TSU KOON)
Chief Minister of Penang

Contents

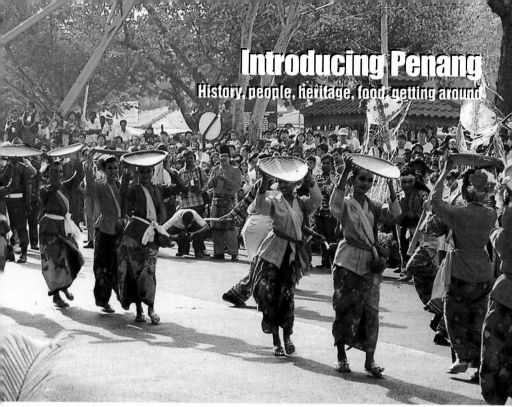

Penang has a long history of accepting people from different cultures. At this crossroads of major civilisations, communities of Arabs, Burmese, Chinese, Eurasians, Malays, Indians, Indonesians and Thais have all come through her island's historic port to make their homes here. Today, George Town, the island's modern capital, with its sizable historic centre, and bordered by forested hills and sandy beaches, is a continuing attraction for travellers from all over the world.

For more than two centuries, travellers have stopped at the port of Penang to view its natural and cultural attractions, savour its food, and meet its people. Located in the centre of Asia's three most densely populated nations - China, India and Indonesia - it has absorbed migrants from all three regions, to become one of Asia's most thriving cross-cultural centres.

Penang combines the attractions of an international beach resort, a uniquely multicultural heritage and food centre, with a go-ahead reputation as the 'Silicon Valley of the East'. Today, over 3 million visitors make their way to this cosmopolitan state of just over a million and a quarter people, every year. But the best is yet to come: at the turn of the millennium, Penang is set to emerge as the most culturally diverse heritage destination in the East.

It is said that British and other English-speaking travellers visit Penang for its heritage city's Chinatown and colonial attractions, the French for its heritage and cultural diversity, the Germans for eco-tourism and rural sights, the Taiwanese and Singaporeans for cheap dining and temple wonders, and the Japanese for golfing and shopping. In general, cultural tourism and eco-tourism are growing interests, but Penang's largely English-speaking communities have also made education and medical tourism a major attraction.

Inevitably, the tourism industry will have an impact on the sensibilities of the local people. But, decent dress, as well as a respect for

Captain Francis Light, "Malaysia's first British pioneer"

local cultures, will go a long way to make the visitor's stay truly enjoyable.

History

Francis Light established Britain's trading post in Penang in 1786 for trade between India, China and the archipelago. Although Light negotiated unsuccessfully with the Sultan of Kedah for the lease of Penang island to the East India Company, he went ahead to take possession of the island, making it the first British settlement in the Malay Peninsula. The occupation was later legalised through gunboat diplomacy. In 1800, an additional strip, on the other side of the channel, and named Province Wellesley by Light, was acquired.

Penang Island was known to the locals as *Pulau Kasatu*. Francis Light called it "Prince of Wales Island", but this name never really caught on, though the capital, George Town, named after Britain's then reigning monarch, King George III, remains. Admin-

istratively, Penang was part of India before becoming a member of the Straits Settlements, along with Malacca and Singapore.

Initially famed for clove and nutmeg, Penang gradually turned to sugar and coconut as cash crops. Pepper was imported from Aceh in Sumatra, in the Indonesian Archipelago, for re-export. With British intervention in the Malay states, Penang became rich from the tin mines in the neighbouring state of Perak.

As Britain's only strategic port of call in the Straits of Malacca, Penang was soon linked by ship to Madras, Rangoon, Medan and Singapore. It served as an entrepot for the south of Thailand, the north of peninsular Malaya, and the north of Sumatra - a region known today as the Indonesia-Malaysia-Thailand Growth Triangle (IMT-GT).

In the early 20th century, Penang prospered from tin, rubber and shipping. The European planters and Chinese towkays (business leaders) made their money in the plantations and mines of the other Northern States but built their mansions in George Town and sent their children to school here.

By the 1930s, more than forty steamship lines connected Penang to the rest of the world, and there were already "Flying Boat" services to London and Singapore. Penang had become an entertainment centre, with cabarets, cinemas, amusement parks and gambling establishments. The popularity of the turf club led to the ruin of many rich families whose sons were tempted to bet on slow horses and fast women.

At the start of the Japanese Occupation (1941-1945), the streets

of George Town were shelled by Japanese war planes and the Allied Forces did even greater damage to the city's historic buildings. However, much of the original colonial architecture did survive - hence its reputation as one of the most intact heritage cities in Asia today.

George Town, which has the oldest municipal history in the country, was awarded City status by royal charter on 1st January 1957. On August 31 that year, Penang became a member state in a newly independent Federation of Malaya, and, when Britain finally withdrew from Singapore, North Borneo and Sarawak in 1963, Penang became part of an enlarged Federation of Malaysia. Penang state is now made up of two municipalities - the Municipal Council of Penang Island (MPPP) and the Municipal Council of Seberang Perai (MPSP).

People

With so many visitors arriving and settling on her shores over the past two centuries, Penang may well be one of the most multicultural places in the world.

Eurasian contingent in street celebration

10

Street festival scene at Lebuh Light

In October 1786, Light wrote that "Our inhabitants increase very fast, Choolias, Chinese and Christians. They are already disputing the ground, everyone building as fast as he can".

The initial Malay settlers were soon joined by a wide range of people, among them are Bengalis, Burmese, Chinese, Ceylonese, Europeans, Gujeratis, Hainanese, Parsis, Pathans, Punjabis, Sindhis and Tamils. Some of the villages formed by these communities survive in urbanised form to the present day.

The historical communities of Armenians and Jews migrated on. But there were also Ambonese, African slaves of unknown origin called Kafirs, and indigenous people from the neighbouring country of Siam, now Thailand, who have since been assimilated into the general population.

Nowadays, many historical sub-communities such as the Straits Chinese, the Jawi Peranakan, the Eurasians, the Indian Muslims and the Siamese make up sizable communities that do not fit neatly into Malaysia's main racial categories of Malays, Chinese and Indians.

The core of the Straits Chinese are descendants of the early Chinese immigrant males who coupled with Batak slaves, Siamese, Burmese, Jawi Peranakan or indigenous peoples. The Jawi Peranakan, in Penang called "*Jawi-Pekan*", are descendants of domiciled Indian Muslims or early inter-marriages, where at least one parent is of Arab or Indian Muslim origin - Tamil, Bengali, Malabari, Pathan or Punjabi. The core of the Eurasians are descendants of Phuket's Portuguese Eurasians, but have assimilated Dutch, French and other nationalities.

Almost anywhere you go in Penang, you can get around with the English language. With the first English school and the first English library East of Suez, both established in the 1810s, the state has a long history as a regional centre of education. Today, it has several dozen private colleges.

Heritage

The city of George Town combines immense historical interest with lively neighbourhoods and urban villages which have hitherto provided cheap and relatively decent housing (in contrast to the squatter slums of other big cities in Asia). As a vibrant economic centre, it also sustains numerous small entrepreneurs and family businesses.

The inner city's unique character is a result of the coming together of Penang's diverse heritage, tra-

11

ditions and communities, providing all Penangites with a sense of pride and belonging.

Penang has one of the largest concentrations of prewar buildings in Southeast Asia. Since 1966, these buildings have been protected by default under the Rent Control Act.

Rent control tenants have long been paying rents way below the market levels, causing much bitterness among property owners. The need for a gradual phasing out of rent control, alongside intensive urban rehabilitation, is now an important issue in the state.

Roofscape of George Town's inner city

Penang's living heritage city is now facing a critical period following the repeal of the Rent Control Act on 1 January 2000. The Penang State Government is attempting to ensure that George Town's heritage city and living culture survive this transition. One solution is to get the historic enclave of George Town recognized as a World Heritage City.

Food

"It seems that at any given time, one half of Penang is cooking for the other half to eat", remarked a visitor. Penangites eat around the clock, and they like to eat something different every day. Fortunately, that's not difficult. Penang's cultural diversity is reflected *par excellence* in its cuisine - a mixture of Chinese, Indian, Malay, Siamese, European, and everything in between.

Penang *Nyonya* food, different from the Malacca and Singapore types, is renowned as one of Malaysia's finest cuisines. The Nyonyas of Penang spiced up

Chinese cooking with the sweet, sour and spicy elements of Thai food. They also concocted rich, deluxe versions of Malay curries and desserts - more coconut milk, more fine ingredients, more of everything - which now provide truly superb dining for both visitors and locals.

Another historical contribution to Penang cuisine was made by the Hainanese from China's Hainan Province who worked as domestic servants for European families. They began developing their own brand of "Western food" and went

into the restaurant business with it.

Penang is also known for "*Mamak*" food or South Indian Muslim cuisine, such as *nasi kandar, nasi briyani* and *murtabak* and an assortment of breads like *thosei, capati* and *roti canai,* all of which should be doused down with *teh tarik* (tea freshly brewed and "pulled").

For international restaurant cuisine, you have a choice of Italian, French, German, Cantonese, Szechuan and North Indian. Most

Built to order food courts offering a wide range of Penang hawker foods are popular eating places

Teh - or kopi-tarik or "pulled" tea or coffee froths the drinks and is popular. *Cappucino*, anyone?

It all began in 19th century when Penang had a large transient male population from India, China and elsewhere in the archipelago. Most of these were petty traders and indigent coolies; it was only the wealthy merchants who could afford to take wives and maintain families. So it was that a food culture developed where itinerant male hawkers sold food to the largely male population.

Some were traditional foods adapted to street hawking; others were simply "cooked up". The result was a large array of cuisines, including cultural hybrids, such as Chinese noodles with Indian sweet potato sauce (*Kelinga*, or, "Indian" Mee).

Penang has become so renowned for its hawker food that "*Penang Hokkien Mee*", "Penang *Laksa*", "Penang *Char Koay Teow*", "Penang *Sar Hor Fun*" and the like are sold all over the region, especially in Singapore and Kuala Lumpur's satellite towns where there are colonies of Penangites.

Penang's hawker food tradition is so popular that it doesn't need to be defended - at least for the time being. It is promoted abroad, for example, at the biannual "Penang Week in Adelaide", Australia, and other events. Even hotels incorporate hawker cuisine into their menus and buffet offerings.

Getting Around

From the island's Bayan Lepas International Airport, you can take a taxi to the city centre and the beach hotels. Fares are controlled via a coupon system, costing from RM10 for nearby Bayan Lepas to RM48 for Teluk Bahang over 30 kilometres away.

The ferry terminal at Butterworth

hotels offer lavish buffets that combine western soups, salads and meat cuts, Malay curries, Hainanese mee and fried rice, Italian pasta and a choice of local and western desserts.

Penang is called "Hawker's Paradise" for several reasons. The hawkers are strongly supported by Penangites, who mostly find it easier and cheaper to eat out - any time of the day or night - than to cook at home. People come from all over Malaysia and Singapore just to binge on hawker food in Penang. More and more people, either needing a part-time job or simply preferring to be self-employed, have begun to sell hawker food. The formula is simple: learn a dish, perfect it, add your own unique twist, set up a push-cart, and, there you go - you have become another member of Penang's hawker community.

The ubiquitousness of hawkers along the streets of Penang has been a delight for food lovers and a big headache for the municipal authorities for over a hundred years.

connects directly to the KTM national railway line which links the state to Bangkok, Ipoh, Kuala Lumpur and Singapore.

A north-south expressway along the west coast of Peninsular Malaysia, as well as an east-west counterpart linking it to the east coast, provides Penang's road connection to Peninsular Malaysia, Thailand in the north and Singapore in the south. From and to the mainland, the motorist can opt for a cross-channel ferry crossing at Butterworth, or drive along the 13.5-kilometre bridge further south, to the island portion of the state.

The transport symbol of Penang is the trishaw, passenger-carrying tricycles, which among its other uses, take children to school and old women to the market. Introduced in 1941, they steadily replaced the rickshaw, for which no new licences were granted after 1953.

The word jinricksha is made up of three Chinese characters meaning "man, energy, car". In short, the rickshaw is the original

Children taking a trishaw to school

"man-powered vehicle", and offers pollution-free transport in a pedestrianised city centre.

Before the war, other common vehicles included the handcart, the gharry or backney carriage, the private horse carriage, the donkey cart, the bullock cart, the trolley bus, the motorcar and the lorry. Bicycles were the predominant mode of private transport but have now been replace by motorised traffic.

Electric tramways, started in 1906 and discontinued in the 1960's, are fondly remembered.

The number of locally licenced cars has risen from four in 1904, to 2,615 cars in 1940 and 1 million today, with the number steadily increasing.

British tourists who come to Penang often remark that the people drive on the "correct" side of the road, i.e. the left. However, do not expect to find British road order here. Penang drivers move rather like a school of fish. They meander to where there is room to move with a lot of give-and-take,

but as they rarely travel at more than 20 miles per hour, accidents are mostly minor. For those used to more disciplined ways, it is best to leave the driving to a taxi or bus driver, unless you want to take a motoring trip out of town, or "outstation", as is said locally.

Taxis have recently started to have meters on them, but it is still better to fix the charge to your destination in advance.

Large passenger cruise ships call at Swettenham Pier, as do smaller cruise ships plying between Penang and Langkawi in Kedah, or Medan in Sumatra, Indonesia.

The Penang ferry terminal was built over 40 years ago, but the cross-channel ferry service linking the island to the peninsula is efficient besides providing a memorable experience.

Adjacent to the mainland ferry terminal, long-distance bus lines connect to most major towns within the peninsular and into Thailand and Singapore to the north and south respectively. On the island side the Red, Blue,

Green and Yellow bus lines can be used to reach most parts of the state.

All island bus lines pass through the main bus transport terminal at KOMTAR which has buses going to all parts of the island.

If you want to join a sight-seeing tour, a few standard packages are available. The most popular bus coach tours take you on "round-the-island" or "hill-and-temple" tours. If you wish to venture out of your hotel for half a day, you can also take the city tour, but if you have more time, it is best to see George Town on foot and by trishaw, since most attractions are concentrated within walking distance.

There are two American Express Heritage Express trails, which you can explore on foot or by trishaw. The first starts from Fort Cornwallis, and the second from the Penang Museum.

The Proton national car makes up most of Penang taxis. Shown here are those found at the Jalan Ria taxi stand near Komtar.

Note: *Jalan* (road) means a main road in Penang. *Lebuh* (street) refers to a road. *Lebuhraya* is an avenue though the correct word is simply, lebuh. *Lorong* is a lane. In other words, the hierarchy of streets in Penang seems to have been inverted. By right, a *lebuh* is larger than a *jalan*, but here it is the other way round.

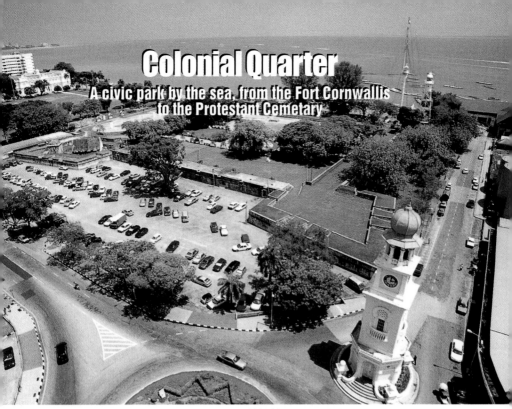

Follow the footsteps of Francis Light - from Fort Cornwallis, which marks the point where he landed, to Government House, where he lived, to his memorial, and finally, on to the Protestant cemetery where he was buried. The colonialists gone, it is the locals who enjoy this civic park where many of George Town's public institutions are located today.

Your tour of George Town can begin from Fort Cornwallis, which is physically and historically the cornerstone of George Town. The Fort lies at the north eastern tip of the triangular cape on which most of the city of George Town is built.

The majority of the residences and government offices of the early European officers were built in and around this part of the cape where full vantage of the sea view and refreshing breezes could be enjoyed. However, although this north beach area constituted the European quarter of Penang's trading port, there was no great buffer between it and the "native" part of town. While few of the European bungalows remain, the north beach has evolved into a civic park, where the courts, the library, religious and other public buildings are to be found.

The star-shaped **Fort Cornwallis** marks the point where Francis Light and his crew landed in 1786 to "take possession" of the island.

At first a nibong stockade was erected, but this was quickly replaced by a brick fort. Old paintings and postcards depict Fort Cornwallis as a number of buildings surrounded by a moat, but only the original Christian chapel and a gunpowder magazine remain. Nevertheless, it is the most intact fort in West Malaysia though systematic excavation has yet to be carried out.

The current interpretation found at the fort represents a form of "reverse) colonisation" in which the British fort has been appropriated

15

for a display of Malay culture. A small admission fee is charged. Outside the entrance a sign indicates the starting point of the **first American Express Heritage Trail**.

Among the cannons placed at the ramparts, the most famous is the **Seri Rambai** (originally "Si Rambai"), a demi-cannon which is inscribed with the seal of the Dutch East India Company. Since 1605, this Dutch cannon has undergone an incredible journey. It was presented to the Sultan of Johore, captured by invading Acehnese, given away to the Sultan of Selangor, and finally seized by the Madras Native Infantry and brought to Penang. The cannon is now viewed as a fertility symbol, and flowers are offered here by local women to enhance their child-bearing prospects. Quite inexplicable, as it would mean the cannon was believed to have power over the spouses of these optimistic women!

The fort is bordered by an Espla-

City Hall at the Esplanade

nade to the north, and the Padang, a large green field, to the west.

The **Padang** was used as a site for firing practice by the sepoy regiments stationed at the fort, but as Pax Britannica set in, it was turned over to recreational purposes such as cricket and bowls. The field was also used for public assemblies and parades. From 1890 to 1954, the Manila Band used to play at a band stand formerly situated at the northeast corner. These "Manila men" were the precursors of the Filipino musicians who were brought in to Penang to perform in the island's international hotels. Part of the Padang is now a children's playground with a food court selling Malay food.

Several trees have been planted around the Padang by foreign dignitaries, like the Emperor of Japan, the Governor of Sumatra and the Prime Minister of South Australia. All of these plantings are the *Bunga Tanjung*, a tree with a heavy spreading crown of dark leaves and currently the official tree of the Penang island municipality.

Poised at the far end of the

Padang are the **Town Hall** and the **City Hall**. The latter is the larger building, closer to the sea. Writing in 1880, the Governor of the Straits Settlements, Frederick Weld, eulogised that he "landed in Penang for a ball and supper, which took place at the Town Hall, a building which I had formally opened a few days before, and which is not only a fine building in itself, but which was, on this occasion, decorated with extreme taste".

The Town Hall was originally a social venue for the town's European community. The Chinese called it *Ang Mo Kong Kuan* or European Club. Inside was an assembly hall with a stage as well as a ballroom with adjoining supper rooms. The Penang Library was located here for twenty years or so.

The **City Hall**, which opened in 1903, showcased the impressive Victorian-style public architecture typical of many of Malaysia's turn-of-the-century buildings. Today, the Municipal Councillors still meet in its timber-panelled Council Chambers.

Historically, the **Esplanade** is rather a romantic place. On the fif-

The clocktower at King Edward Place

State Assembly Building facing the Esplanade

is now a secular event participated by Malaysians from all backgrounds. At the far end of the Esplanade is a municipal hawker complex not far from a Cenotaph with brass relief plates dedicated to the memory of those who died in World War One. To the north of this, a bright red buoy in the middle of the sea marks the spot where the Russian Zemschug was sunk by the German cruise ship Der Emden.

South of the Fort are the **State Assembly Buildings** along Lebuh Light. These originally served as the Police Recorders' Courts and then the Magistrate's Courts. They are built in the style of Greek temples, with classical pediments held up by gleaming white colonnades. An administrative block, added in 1890, now serves as the **Immigration Building.**

teenth night of Chinese New Year, a full moon night called *Chap Goh Meh*, the Straits Chinese would gather there, the highlight being a procession of Nyonya-maidens. This was the only opportunity for young men to view the maidens, and then to make inquiries leading to marriage. Before setting off along the waterfront, the maidens, otherwise cloistered in their homes, would alight from their carriages and cars to cast oranges out to sea, wishing for a good match.

Processions and parades are still held several times a year at the Esplanade. Among them are the Chingay festival on Christmas Day, and an orange-throwing competition on *Chap Goh Meh* (around February).

During the *Chingay* festival, teams of men carry and perform stunts with giant flags. The parade evolved from religious festivals but

Going west on Lebuh Light, you see on the right, the city auditorium, the **Dewan Sri Pinang**. It is easily recognizable as a large squarish modern building de-

A dragon dance performance at a Chingay festival

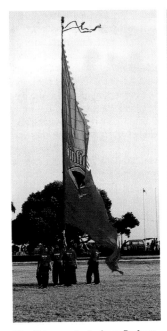

The Chingay starts from Padang Brown in Jalan Datuk Kramat and ends at Padang Kota

signed by Public Works. The building also houses the **Penang State Library** and the **Penang Art Gallery**. The ramps leading up to the building are meant for trolleys carrying props.

At the Lebuh Light detour into Jalan Mesjid Kapitan Keling (Pitt Street) and Jalan Farquhar are the **Court Buildings**. The court-houses were built in 1905 for the Supreme Court, which, at the time, was convened in Penang. For a long time, the Penang Library was accommodated in the wing facing Lebuh Farquhar before it moved to its present premises at the Dewan Sri Pinang.

In the court grounds stands a memorial, raised by public subscription, to James Richardson Logan. James Logan edited the Pinang Gazette while his brother, Abraham, edited the Singapore Free Press. James also founded

George Town's Penaga Trees

Callophyllum inophyllum, Alexandrian Laurel, (in Malay, *Betangur Laut* or *Penaga Laut*)

The original name of the point where George Town was laid out was *Tanjung Penaigre*, as it was spelt on an early map. On 17 July 1786, Captain Light disembarked with his lieutenant on Penang island and wrote in his diary: "Disembarked Lieutenant Gray with the marines upon point Penagger, a low sandy point, covered with wood. Employed clearing the ground".

According to Malay oral tradition, coins were shot by cannon into the thick forest as an incentive to clear the hardwood trees. Several days later they "Dug several wells, found

the Journal of the Indian Archipelago and Eastern Asia, also called Logan's Journals - scholarly publication that could be considered the precursor to the Journal of the Straits Branch, and then of the Malaysian Branch, of the Royal Asiatic Society.

South of the Court Buildings is the St. George's Church, with the Penang State Museum and the Cathedral of the Assumption to its left.

The **St. George's Church** dates from 1818 and is the oldest Anglican Church in the country. The building was designed by Captain Robert Smith, a military engineer whose oil paintings of early Penang are displayed in the Museum. In the grounds of the St. George's Church on Lebuh Farquhar, there

the water indifferent, but stained with the roots of the Penagger which dies red..."

Once cleared, the town was established and peopled predominantly with immigrants. The memory of the penaga tree faded from memory. Today, Penang Malays simply refer to the cape as "Tanjung".

This led the Municipal Council some years ago to declare the *Bunga Tanjung* (*Mimusops elengi*) the official tree of George Town, even to the extend of ruling that no other tree should be planted on official occasions. Meanwhile, the real tree from which Tanjung Penaga derived its name is nowhere to be found in its original habitat around Fort Cornwallis. In George Town, a few specimens survive at the Residency and the Penang Botanic Gardens.

stands a memorial in the form of a Greek temple with a marble slab inscribed. "In Memory of FRANCIS LIGHT, Esquire, Who first established this island as an English Settlement & was many years Governor. Born in the County of Suffolk in England and died October 21st 1794."

The **Penang State Museum** recently reopened after a major renovation. Exhibits include those organised according to Penang's communities, their customs and costumes; historic places such as the harbour, Fort Cornwallis, and streets of Penang; municipal history; the Penang Riots; the Japanese Occupation; houses of worship; and traditional trades.

There are special rooms showcasing the paintings of Captain

The Logan memorial can be found on the Court Building grounds

The Francis Light Memorial with St. Georges Church behind it

Stained glass at the Cathedral of the Assumption

Robert Smith and the engravings of William Daniell, as well as rooms for straits Chinese material heritage, in particular a bridal chamber. Among the few original collections showcased in this museum is a collection of handwritten Qur'ans and old Malay weapons from the family of the late Dato' Haji Fathil Basheer. A bronze statue of Captain Francis Light stands outside the Museum building.

The Penang Museum is housed in the former premises of the Penang Free School which was constructed in two stages, in 1896 and 1906. During the Second World War, bombs fell on the older half, leaving only half a building today. The Penang Heritage Trust runs a small shop there selling souvenirs, books, postcards and antiques. The shop is located in a former Penang Hill railway carriage at one end of the yard. Part of the proceeds goes towards the Penang Heritage Trust. The **American Express Heritage Trail 2** starts here.

The **Cathedral of the Assumption** was formerly the Church of the Assumption, so named because the first group of Eurasians from Kedah landed in Penang on the eve of the feast. The present church was built in 1860, and marks the old neighbourhood of the Eurasian community. In fact a

few Eurasian homes are still to be found behind the church, on Argus Lane.

Opposite the Cathedral is Penang's Catholic secondary school for girls. The **Convent of the Holy Infant Jesus**, better known as the Convent Light Street, was started

Cathedral of the Assumption next to the Penang Museum at Lebuh Farquhar

19

Penang court buildings at the junction of Lebuh Light and Lebuh Masjid Kapitan Keling

European pioneers such as Francis Light, several early Governors, Raffles' brother-in-law Quintin Dick Thomas, James Scott, David Brown of Glugor Estate, Reverend Hutchings, the Reverend Thomas Beighton of the London Missionary Society and James Richardson Logan. Many of them died of some mysterious tropical fever, which was probably malaria brought about by the widespread clearing of forest. Another personality buried here is a young officer named Thomas Leonowens, whose widow Anna Leonowens became a schoolmistress in Siam and gave inspiration to the story of "The King and I" (recently made into a Hollywood film).

by three French Sisters in 1852. Within the walled complex lies the bungalow of Francis Light, dating back to the 1790s and still in good condition. Next to it is the "**Francis Light Well**". Around 1803, the bungalow was leased to the East India Company for the "Government House", and Stamford Raffles, founder of Singapore, worked here when he was Assistant Secretary for the Penang government from 1805 to 1810. After the Government House was taken over by the Sisters for their convent, they began to add one building after another, turning the place into an extensive complex with a chapel, cloisters for the Sisters, an or-

phanage for unwanted babies, a boarding house for student boarders and blocks of classrooms.

During the Japanese Occupation, several American prisoners were captured from the USS Grenadier in 1943 and incarcerated in "Block C", where their names can be seen scratched on the wall. The Convent Light Street is being lovingly restored and extended with funds raised from the public.

The **Protestant Cemetery** along Jalan Sultan Ahmad Shah deserves to be explored at leisure. Shaded by frangipanni trees, it is the final resting place of Penang's

In 1923, Purcell wrote in his book 'Early Penang': "The modest proportions of Light's tomb have been overshadowed by the monuments of later and lesser defunct ones, but, in 1894, on the centenary of his death, the piety of Penang raised up his broken tombstone and carefully whitewashed it; and there, maybe, the Founder of Penang will rest for another hundred years, disturbed only by the toot of motor horns, until Penang's piety in 1994 remembers him again, restores his tombstone, and gives it another coat of whitewash."

In 1994, Purcell's statement proved prophetic when the Penang Heritage Trust, with funding from the French plantation company SOCFIN, organised the whitewashing and re-inking of the tombs at the Protestant Cemetery.

Today, a signboard near the entrance tells you the location of the tombs of Light and other notables. On the southern wall of the cemetery, a small entrance leads to the Catholic cemetery and the St. Francis Xavier Church.

One of the many corridor hallways in Convent Light Street in Lebuh Light

The Historic Port Settlement
Little India, Mosques and Kongsis along the waterfront

The grid laid out by Francis Light is a lively centre of ethnic eating-places and retail shops in the streets, as well as squares and boulevards linked to the waterfront. This is where most of Penang's oldest mosques, temples and *kongsis* are concentrated - jewels of architecture linked by surviving early vernacular shophouses. The association buildings could be used to interpret George Town's past, each serving as an "open museum of migration" for the history of a particular migrant group, adding up to a vivid picture of Penang's multicultural society.

Like many colonial ports, Penang had its colonial quarter and its ethnic enclaves, but here they were laid out so close to each other as to afford little segregation.

The earliest commercial centre was a grid bounded by Lebuh Light, Lebuh Pantai (Beach Street), Lebuh Chulia and Jalan Masjid Kapitan Keling (Pitt Street) to the north, east, south and west, respectively. With Lebuh Bishop, Lebuh Gereja (Church Street), Lebuh China and Lebuh Pasar (Market Street), as intermediate streets connecting Jalan Masjid Kapitan Keling to Lebuh Pantai from east to west, and Lebuh King and Lebuh Penang, to connect Lebuh Light with Lebuh Chulia from north to south.

Lebuh Light was reserved for officers' homes and public buildings. Lebuh Bishop was intended for the presbytery of the bishop of the Eurasian's Catholic Church, originally on Lebuh Gereja. Lebuh China was marked out for the Chinese and led from the waterfront to the Chinese temple at the Jalan Masjid Kapitan Keling end. And Lebuh Pasar was reserved for the market by the sea.

Lebuh Chulia was occupied by Indian Muslims. To the south, Lebuh Armenian was meant for the Armenians (but they soon relocated to Lebuh Bishop), while Lebuh Acheh (Acheen Street) was the street for the Achehnese from Sumatra.

By 1908, the Europeans had already long moved out to the suburbs

Ceramic birds and flowers gilding the roof of the Yap Kongsi building on Lebuh Armenian

and a European visitor regarded the commercial town pretty much as a "native quarter".

"All the streets west of Beach Street [Lebuh Pantai] follow a rectangular design, which renders the task of finding one's way about the town simplicity itself, and within those streets nearest to Beach Street are to be found the best studies of Oriental arts and industries. At the (southern half), the proverbial industry of the Chinese is well emphasised; for, long after his European rival in business has not only gone home for the day, but retired for the night as well, the Chinaman has his shop brightly lit up with great hanging lamps, and an army of assistants, clerks, and coolies are hard at work."

"And then there are Asiatics of other nationalities, who have, metaphorically "pitched their tents' in Pinang in order to gain a livelihood - the Indian money-changers, whose stalls are to be seen on every pavement; the Chetty money-lenders, whose habitations are to be found clustered together in a row in Pinang Street and King Street, the Sinhalese silver-ware dealer and

vendor of lace; the "Bombay merchant', who stocks everything from curios to cottons... *All these and more are to be met with in Pinang, which is nothing if not cosmopolitan*".

Today, this grid is called "Historic Commercial District - Little India" under the city's conservation guidelines. You will find a large number of very modest squat houses, which are the first generation brick shophouses in this area, dating from the first half of the 19th century.

Little India

The old commercial centre is strongly associated with "Little India", which properly refers to the Indian quarter with rows of Indian shops concentrated along Lebuh Pasar (Market Street), Lebuh Penang, Lebuh Queen and an adjacent section of Lebuh Chulia. This quarter has both Muslim and Hindu places of worship - the Kapitan Keling Mosque, the Nagore Shrine and the Mahariamman Temple.

When most other old shopping areas are declining because of increasing competition from the

new shopping centres mushrooming all over Penang, Little India has done very well because it offers specialised ethnic shopping such as spices, *saris, sarongs* and stainless steel ware for Indian food. A street festival is held here on the night of *Deepavali* (around November).

Little India has also witnessed a flourishing of South Indian restaurants, such as **Meena's**, **Sushi's** and **Kaliaman's** all along Lebuh Penang. Banana leaf rice, that is, rice and curries served on banana leaf, is usually taken with *papadam* crackers and a fresh yoghurt *lassi* drink. These and other restaurants on Lebuh Pasar also serve *thosei*, a healthy, rice and bean flour pancake. **Woodlands** is a vegetarian restaurant offering a wonderful array of pancakes and side dishes.

Apart from these, many roadside *"Mamak* stalls" are open for breakfast, lunch, dinner and supper. The Indian Muslims stallkeepers are popularly addressed as "*Mamak*", which means uncle. They have mastered the art of "throwing" the *roti canai* dough and "pulling" the *teh tarik*. The bread is served optionally with dhal while the tea is invariable made thick and foamy, white and sweet.

Dawood Restaurant, occupying an early 1960s art moderne building, is the place for authentic Tamil Muslim food, such as *nasi briyani*, a rich spiced rice dish originating from Persia, with or without meat, *khurma* and *dhal*. In the evenings, a *capati* bread stall in front adds to the food variety.

Jalan Masjid Kapitan Keling

The East India Company allotted land along this street, formerly called Pitt Street, for the respective communities to build their houses of worship. Penang's "Street of Harmony" actually starts from the St. George's Church on Lebuh Farquhar (in the colonial quarter) at the northern end, and proceeds southwards to the Goddess of Mercy Temple, the Mahariamman Temple on Lebuh Queen, the Kapitan Keling Mosque, past the Khoo Kongsi, down to the Acheen Street Mosque at the southern end of the road. Jalan Masjid Kapitan Keling is lined with flower-sellers, money-changes and jewellers, with a few antique shops and coin and stamp dealers in between.

The **Goddess of Mercy Temple**, also called the Pitt Street Temple or *Kuan Yin Teng*, is situated along Jalan Masjid Kapitan Keling at its junction with Lebuh China. The temple is dedicated to two virgin goddesses, the Buddhist *Kuan Yin* or Goddess of Mercy, and *Ma Chor Poh*, the patron saint of seafarers. The temple was founded in 1801 on a piece of land granted

by the East India Company. The original name for the temple was **Kong Hock Keong** (Cantonese-Hokkien Temple), as it was jointly established by both language-speaking groups.

Undoubtedly the most popular Chinese temple in Penang, the *Kuan Yin Teng* is particularly congested on the first and fifteenth day of each lunar month. On the Goddess of Mercy's feast days, on the 19th day of the second, sixth and ninth month of the lunar calendar, puppet shows and Chinese operas are staged. The lovely square is always a centre of bustling activity, with temple hawkers, the burning of joss papers and other activities. At one corner of the square is an octagonal well, once a public well for the Chinese community.

The temple is considered to be of such geomantic significance that when the Malayan Railway building with its clocktower was built in 1907, the Chinese community saw it as a British conspiracy

against them. It was said that the temple's pair of stone lions who loved to gambol out to the water's edge at night, were now deprived of their favorite pastime.

Across the road from the Goddess of Mercy Temple is a newspaper office. The 1906 building was actually purpose built as the Government Opium & Spirit Farm Offices. It served as a godown and dispensary for chandu, or cooked opium, and samsoo, an alcohol distilled from rice and sugar. For a long time the Straits Settlements government derived much revenue from tendering out opium and samsoo licences, but due to considerable lobbying from the Anti-Opium movement and others, it was no longer regarded morally acceptable for the colonial government to be profiting handsomely from drugs and alcohol.

Lebuh China is presently home to a collection of legal offices, trading and commercial companies, with a number of coffee shops selling Chinese food, supplemented by hawker stalls in the evening.

The **Mahamariamman Temple** was built in 1833 and is renovated every few decades or so. The temple has an entrance on Lebuh Queen (an additional road connecting Jalan Gereja to Jalan Chulia) and a gate on Jalan Masjid Kapitan Keling which is kept closed. Located in the heart o f Little India, the street surface in front is usually painted with a traditional *kolam* diagram. The Thaipusam procession begins here, as does the *Vijayadasami* festival (around October), which features a wooden chariot taking the deity out on a tour of Little India.

The **Kapitan Keling Mosque** is

Festival Day at the Kuan Yin Temple on Jalan Kapitan Keling

the most prominent historic mosque in Penang. In 1801, the East India Company granted a large piece of land to the "Mohammedan Church". Kapitan Keling, that is, the Captain of the Kelings or the appointed head of the South Indian community, collected subscriptions and brought builders and materials from India to build the first permanent mosque. The old mosque was a rectangular building with a hipped roof, encircled by a stone bench. It was situated in a small compound in the midst of a large burial ground and urban village, from which rentals went towards its upkeep and other charities.

The Kapitan Keling Mosque from Jalan Masjid Kapitan Keling

In 1905, the colonial government formed the Mohamedan and Hindoo Endowment Board and took over the administration of the trust lands in the interest of managing some of the most valuable real estate in the municipality. They then began an extensive urban renewal programme, replacing the squatter housing with social housing designed by European architects. The mosque was enlarged into a Moghul revival mosque with onion shaped domes and turrets. After several major renovations, the present form finally arrived in the 1930s.

The Kapitan Keling Mosque is the place of worship of the Indian Muslim community who have lived and worked around the mosque for over two hundred years. Among the Indian Muslims with shops here are jewellers, money-changers, textile dealers, restauranters, food hawkers, newspaper vendors, stevedores and ship-chandlers. Unlike the modern drive-in mosque which are mainly frequented on Fridays, the Kapitan Keling Mosque is used by worshippers five times a day, seven days a week. The mosque is full on Fridays and overflows during the Muslim celebration of *Hari Raya Aidil Fitri* and *Hari Raya Haji*.

The Kapitan Keling Mosque, the Acheen Street Mosque, and the area to the south of Lebuh Acheh, belong to another precinct under the conservation guidelines called the "Mosque and Clan House Enclave". Commissioned by the Tourism Ministry, an Action Plan for the area roughly bounded by Lebuh Pasar, Lebuh Acheh, Lebuh Pantai and Jalan Masjid Kapitan Keling was drawn up by South Australian Heritage Consultants & Contractors, who were also involved in dilapidation surveys of the Kapitan Keling Mosque and Suffolk House.

Lebuh Armenian

At the southern end of Jalan Masjid Kapitan Keling (where it intersects Jalan Armenian) is the **Yap Kongsi**, a clan house for preserving the ancestral tablets of the clan's ancestors. In front of the Yap Kongsi lies a square where you can usually find a flock of pigeons and Muhammad's blue pushcart selling *teh tarik* and ginger tea. On your left is a corner coffee shop with a little rounded balcony next to which is the entrance to the **Tua Pek Kong Temple** (called *Hock Teik Cheng Sin Temple*). Turning west onto Lebuh Armenian, you will come to a curve in the road.

The shophouse at **120 Armenian Street**, with its facade limewashed indigo blue, is **Dr. Sun Yat Sen's Penang base**. Dating from just after 1875, this Straits Chinese residential terrace house maintains a heritage interior complete with carved screens, 1920s furnishings and an inner courtyard garden. Since 1926, this house had been in the family of a licenced gun dealer, the late Ch'ng Teong Swee. Today, it is the home of conservationist writer, Khoo Salma Nasution.

Dr. Sun Yat Sen and his party orchestrated a famous event of the 1911 Chinese Revolution from his Penang base. Following the move of the headquarters of the Southeast Asian division of the Tung Meng Hooi party from his villa in Singapore to this terrace house,

The Yap Kongsi at the junction of Lebuh Armenian, Jalan Mesjid Kapitan Keling and Medan Cannon

Dr. Sun Yat Sen, on 13th November 1910, convened the famous "Penang Meeting" at his new base. It was an Emergency General Meeting convened to plan the Canton Uprising which took place in Guangzhou on the 29th day of the 3rd month of the lunar calendar (27 April 1911). A fund raising campaign was launched; in only two days Dr. Sun managed to raise more than 8,000 Straits Dollars on the spot. Money also poured in from Chinese communities in Canada, British Malaya, the Dutch East Indies, French Indo-China, Thailand and the United States. "The Overseas Chinese are the mother of the Chinese Revolution", was Dr. Sun's famous quote.

Of the "72 Martyrs" memorialized at Hwang Hwa Kang, Guangzhou in China, many came from British Malaya and the Dutch Indies. Among the martyrs were "gifted poets, distinguished writers, popular journalists, skilled workers and farmers". Following the Wuchang Uprising in October, dubbed the "Double Tenth Revolution", Dr. Sun became the first

Provisional President of the new Republic. Today, he is widely regarded as "the father of modern China".

Dr. Sun first came to Penang in 1906, and returned each year until 1911. During his sojourns in Penang, he stayed at the homes of his many wealthy supporters, where he was lavishly treated to wine, woman and song. His main residence was at 400 Jalan Dato' Keramat (since demolished).

The Penang supporters of the Chinese Revolution were led by Goh Say Eng who started the Penang Branch of the Tung Meng Hooi in 1906, the Penang Philomatic Society in 1908, and together with Dr. Sun co-founded the Kwong Wah Jit Poh in 1910. The Kwong Wah Jit Poh is the oldest Chinese-language newspaper in Malaysia, and was first published from 120 Armenian Street.

At the junction of Lebuh Armenian and Lebuh Acheh is the only neighbourhood park in the inner city. There are plans to make it child and disabled friendly.

Four doors away from Dr. Sun's Penang base is the **Heritage Centre, Penang.** The detached bungalow housing the Centre used to be the home of Syed Mohd. Alatas, an Arab pepper trader from Acheh.

The merchants of Penang, Muslims as well as Straits Chinese, invested in pepper plantations on the east coast of Sumatra from the 1840s until the Dutch invaded Acheh in the 1870s and disrupted the trade. Syed Mohd. Alatas was one of the affected traders who then supported the Achehnese resistance by smuggling arms to Acheh. He was also the leader of the Red Flag secret society based in Lebuh Acheh until the 1890s, after which his son took over. Syed Mohd. Alatas lived here with his first wife, of Malay royal descent. He stayed with his second wife, a Straits Chinese, at a bungalow on Lebuh Carnarvon which is now the premises of Li Teik Seah. His second wife was a daughter of Khoo Tiang Poh, the leading pepper and shipping merchant of that time, who was also a leader of the Hokkien secret

120 Lebuh Armenian

society.

From the 1930s, the **Syed Alatas Mansion** was used as a junkyard run by the Indian Chettiar scrap collectors, several decades ago. Then it was acquired by the Municipal Council to be demolished for road-widening. In 1993, it became the subject of a pilot restoration project financed by federal, state and municipal governments, and headed by conservation architect Didier Repellin, head conservator of Lyon. Today, the premises are still owned by the Municipal Council, but the Heritage Centre is run by the State Government. The Penang Organic Farm runs a vegetarian restaurant at the back, called Green Rhythm.

The Syed Alatas Mansion, restored in 1993 with French assistance, is now the premises of the Heritage Centre, Penang

Lebuh Acheh

The original name "Acheen Street" comes from the old name for Acheh, that is, "Acheen". The name has been translated as Lebuh Acheh, but at times, just to be confusing, it has also been re-translated into "Acheh Street", which has no basis whatsoever in municipal history.

The entrance to the Acheen Street Mosque from Lebuh Aceh is dominated by its minaret

Lebuh Acheh used to be a centre for Arab and Achehnese traders. In the mid-19th century, there were about 300 traders staying here at any one time. The native trade between Penang and Acheh was disrupted by the Dutch invasion of Acheh. In place of the Achehnese, the Rawa, Minang and Talu people from West Sumatra began to dominate the scene. The Rawas traditionally run the printing presses and bookshops in Lebuh Acheh.

At the same time, the traffic in pilgrims gave Lebuh Acheh a second lease of life in the early 20th century. Syed Ahmad Al-Mashoor's Juddah Pilgrimage agency was the licenced local agent of Mansfield & Co., which chartered Blue Funnel Line ships to the port of Jeddah and thence on to Mecca to perform the Haj.

Lebuh Acheh became the "Second Jeddah", with inns, food stalls and shops catering to Muslim travellers. This period came to an end when the pilgrimage ship was replaced by the flying ship, i.e. the aeroplane, and the business was taken over by the official Pilgrimage Fund (*Tabung Haji*).

The **Acheen Street Mosque**, or Masjid Melayu Lebuh Acheh, was founded by Tengku Syed Hussain Al-Idid, an Arab merchant-prince from Acheh. He settled in Penang in 1792, during the time of Francis Light, together with his brother and their large clans. Tengku Syed Hussain's son became Sultan of Acheh for a few years before he was ousted by the old Sultan with the help of the British. This was the prelude to the signing of the Anglo-Dutch treaty of 1824.

Daily visitors at the Khoo Kongsi on Lebuh Cannon

The vernacular style mosque from 1808 remained basically unmodified except for the Moorish arcade added at the turn of the century. The minaret was struck by lightning in 1997, and the mosque was recently restored with French technical assistance. The compound houses around the mosque are part of the mid-19th century Arab village.

Walking up Lebuh Cannon, you will find the inconspicuous entrance to the **Khoo Kongsi**. This clan temple is probably the most celebrated historic attraction in George Town. The Leong San Tong Khoo Kongsi (the Dragon Mountain Hall Khoo Company) was a clan association formed in Penang in 1835 by immigrants hailing from the Khoo clan village, not far from Xiamen in Fujian, China. In 1851 they purchased the site, built housing for clan members and used an existing building as their temple. During the

Penang riots of 1867, the Khoo clan led the predominantly Hokkien (Fujian) Tua Pek Kong secret society, based at the Tua Pek Kong Temple next door. After secret societies were banned, the Khoos returned to respectability. Khoo Thean Teik, the former secret society leader, became one of the founders of the Chinese Town Hall.

Thus in the 1890s, the Khoo leaders began the project of building a grand clan temple at Medan Cannon, dedicated to the clan's patron deities and serving to house the ancestral tablets. The first temple built on the site was burnt down, allegedly struck by lightning. The present temple, completed in 1906, is a monument of Chuan Chew architecture, apparently more elaborate than anything of that period and style built in China.

A "*kongsi*", which means partner-

ship, or company, is something like a Chinese guild, set up by immigrant groups for their mutual benefit. The five Great Clans of 19th-century Penang - the Khoo, Cheah, Yeoh, Lim and Tan - were Hokkien-speaking, originating from Fujian province in China. Each clan formed a kongsi and built their clanhouses within a stone's throw of each other. In the vicinity of the Khoo Kongsi at Medan Cannon, the Cheah Kongsi is located at Lebuh Armenian, the Yeoh at Lebuh Chulia, the Lim at Lebuh Ah Quee, and the Tan at **Seh Tan Court**, just off Lebuh Pantai.

The joint temple of the five clans, the **Tua Pek Kong Temple**, is located at Lebuh Armenian. In addition, there is also the Boon San Tong Khoo Kongsi, a branch of the main Khoo Kongsi, at Lebuh Victoria.

There are seven temples in all

Entrance to the Mahamariamman Temple on Lebuh Queen

Interior of Mahamariamman Temple on Lebuh Queen

belonging to the Five Great Clans, and a walking tour of these could well be devised for groups. Like the Khoo Kongsi, most of the Kongsi buildings are large temples set in courtyards, surrounded by shophouses and accessible only through narrow gateways. This unique defensive layout of the Hokkien Kongsis in Penang helped them survive the secret society feuds of the 19th century. The Kongsis come alive during the Winter Solstice celebrations (around December) when the clans gather to offer respect to ancestors with food, drink and prayers.

Nowadays, the Khoo Kongsi is so much regarded as a tourist attraction, that many Khoos no longer identify with it as their clan house. The Khoo Kongsi's original function, as a guild and temple embodying the ideals of Confucian piety, social justice and welfare for the clan, has been somewhat obscured over the years. There are plans to turn the Khoo Kongsi into some sort of tourist village, and it is hoped by many that this enterprise will be carried out with re-

spect for the building's legacy. From another side gate of the Khoo Kongsi, you can get back to Lebuh Armenian. And from here, you can take a walk through Lorong Soo Hong, which was named after Khoo Soo Hong, one of the senators on the Khoo Kongsi board in 1851. You will then come to Lebuh Ah Quee, where, an attractive old building, once a Muslim school for the teaching of Arabic language, Qur'an and Islamic law, can be found at the junction.

Walking through Pitt Lane back to Lebuh Chulia and you will see the Nagore Shrine directly in front of you. The eastern section of Lebuh Chulia, near the Nagore Shrine, is lined with Muslim shops selling *sarongs*, *batik* and carpets.

The **Nagore Shrine** is a miniature Moghul monument sitting proudly at the corner of Lebuh Chulia and Lebuh King. The site was granted by the East India Company in 1801, on the same day as the grant for the Kapitan Keling Mosque site was issued. The Nagore Shrine was founded by

the Maricars (also known as Mericans) from Tamilnadu. The saint of Nagore, Syed Shahul Hamid, who lived in the 13th century, is the most celebrated saint of South India.

The side wall of the shrine has a built-in arcade with hole-in-the-wall shops, one of them is occupied by a maker of *songkok* (Muslim headgear). These shops are "boutiques" in the original sense, from the Portuguese word *butica* or *boteca* which referred to a "small native shop" in South India or Ceylon.

Lebuh King

Lebuh Chulia, continue back to your starting point by walking through Lebuh King, following the one-way street from south to north. Instead of free-standing temples, the district associations or guilds erected "townhouse temples" conforming to the colonial town layout. When it comes to sheer variety of colonial temple architecture, Lebuh King is the "king of streets".

Stretch of kongsi and association houses along Lebuh King

Proceeding along Lebuh King, you will pass by the **Ku Chen Hooi**, the "Old Castle Association", whose members bear the same surnames as the sworn brothers of the "Three Kingdoms" - Lu Pei, Chang Fei and Kwang Kong.

Walking past the junction with Lebuh Pasar, you will come to the three-storey **Poe Choo Seah** on your right. The premises of this 19th-century Straits Chinese association was opened in 1903. If you are lucky, the elderly caretaker Mr. Khoo may let you in. The building is beautifully maintained and offers a wonderful view of the surrounding roofscapes from the third storey.

Just next to the Poh Choo Seah is the former Ho Seng secret society base, a very broad double-storey building which has been renovated. Directly opposite the Poe Choo Seah is the **Chin Si Tong Soo**, a guild for members with the surname Chin. The building has a three-storey section at

the back decorated with striking "fire gables", as if to challenge the geomantic energy of the Poe Choo Seah situated opposite.

Past the Lebuh China junction and on your right, is the **Lee Shih Chong Soo**, an ensemble of three large shophouses, the middle unit of which is modeled with an eclectic temple facade.

On your left, you will find a fantastic group of temple buildings with fancy gables. Again, most of them date from the 19th century but the taller structures were remodelled after the turn of the century.

The first group consists of three grey brick-faced temples with horse head gables. The first temple is the **Ng See Kah Meow**, for members of the Ng surname, the second is the War Emperor's Temple, the **Wu Ti Meow**, and the third is a Cantonese district temple, the **Toi San Nin Yong Hui Kwon**, formed by Chinese of the Sin Ling dialect group. The squat red struc-

ture next to it is the **Cantonese Tua Pek Kong Temple**. At the corner is the Cantonese district temple, **Chong San Wooi Koon**, with a handsome arcade along Lebuh Gereja.

Past Lebuh Bishop, you will find two buildings for Hakkas from particular Cantonese districts. Both guilds were founded just after 1800 - the **Kar Yin Fooi Koon** was rebuilt with a facade of Shanghai plaster around 1940. The **Tseng Lung Fui Kon** has a unique facade with a double-height archway dated 1922.

Next to the Tseng Lung Fui Kon is an Indian Muslim association at 18 Lebuh King. This is an association of Tamil Muslims from Mutthpehttai.

The **Shaik Dawood Oliyuallah (Mutthuppehtai) Mouluth Sabah**, named after Shaik Dawood, the saint of their home town, was founded around 1914 at 130 Lebuh Chulia and moved to its Lebuh King premises in

Hakka Association building with the rented shophouse premises of the Mutthupehtai Association next to it

1937. The association premises is like a museum frozen in time. The present members and lodgers are mainly elderly men who first came to Penang in the 1930s to work as dock labourers. Their story and historical worldview are illustrated by the several dozen pictures hanging on the wall in the front hall: scenes of fighting from World War I; a portrait of Kemal Attaturk; pictures of the Shaik Dawood shrine in the home village; pictures of Mecca and Madina; photos of King George and Queen Mary; the Barak calendar of 1938 and 1939; pictures of Ali Jinnah; a calendar to celebrate Pakistan's Independence day; and photographs of the members' gatherings in better days.

If you want to continue the tour to Lebuh Pantai, you can walk through Lebuh Gereja (Church Street) to pass the group of green buildings called the **Chung Keng Kooi Temple** on the right.

Chung Keng Kooi was the infamous leader of the 19th Century Hakka-dominated secret society called the Hai San. The society fought in the 19th-century tin wars in Perak, known as the Larut

Wars. The Hai San managed to take over the premises of their rival society, the Ghee Hin triad. Chung Keng Kooi built his magnificent townhouse as well as the family temple on this site in the 1890s. The townhouse cum office, with an inner courtyard, is highly decorated with timber screens, cast iron, and stencilled glass. The family temple has intricate gilded timber screens and ornaments, ceramic decorations, glass chandeliers, portraits and religious items of great historical value. Both buildings are currently protected under a family trust.

Lebuh Pantai

The history of the port is best explored in the area referred to in the conservation guidelines as "Waterfront Business - Financial District". The waterfront recalls the old days of sea travel, when Penang was a favourite port of call.

Lebuh Pantai (Beach Street) was laid by Francis Light along the beach. The two blocks to the east of it were later built on reclaimed land. Many of the buildings here were European offices with retail or wholesale stores on the ground floor. With the opening of the Swettenham Pier and the modernisation of trade and commerce at the dawn of the 20th century, Lebuh Pantai became the address of fashionable commercial buildings designed by European architects.

The former government offices located on Lebuh Downing and Lebuh Pantai were bombed by American B-29s at the close of the Japanese Occupation.

The Survey Office, the one building out of the formerly magnificent quadrangle that survived the bombing, has been converted into

The Immigration building on Jalan Pantai near King Edward Place

the premises of the Muslim Religious Council and the Syariah Court. In the Malay Chambers of Commerce next door, the **Off-Centre Gallery** exhibits the works of artists from Penang's Universiti Science Malaysia (Science University of Malaysia).

Today, Lebuh Pantai is Penang's financial centre with about a dozen banks. The **Hongkong & Shanghai Bank**, the **Standard Chartered Bank**, the **ABN-AMRO Bank** and "the one and only Penang-based bank", the **Ban Hin Lee Bank**, have all refurbished their heritage premises in the last ten years. The rent controlled commercial premises along this street, on the other hand, patiently await similar renovation. In this main commercial street, the traffic pretty much conforms to the usual stereotype of a bustling Asian city. Cars are everywhere and roadside stalls sell cheap clothes and imitation watches, mainly to the hordes of workers who stream out of their air-conditioned offices at lunchtime.

The landmark along Gat Lebuh China (China Street Ghat) is the **Malayan Railway Building**, com-

The Malayan Railway Office building on Gat Lebuh China

pleted in 1907, with a tall clock-tower which not so long ago stood out in the Penang skyline and could be seen by approaching ships. It used to be called "the only railway station without a rail". It was in fact a station hotel with a Railway Restaurant, Bar & Grill and a ticketing booth where you could buy your tickets for the ferry and the train which departed from the station next to the **Butterworth Ferry Terminal** on the mainland. From here, you might want to take the ferry across to catch the train or visit any of the attractions in Seberang Perai

(Province Wellesley), or just ride to and fro for the experience of a ferry cruise.

Pengkalan Weld

Following reclamation of the land east of Lebuh Pantai, Pengkalan Weld (Weld Quay) became the sea-front road of Penang's port settlement.

If you come back by ferry, approaching Penang island, you will have a panoramic view of the water villages, the handsome Malayan Railway Building clock tower, and the turn-of-the-century shipping offices and warehouses (locally known as "godowns"). Along Pengkalan Weld were the offices of European shipping agencies such as Boustead, Schmidt & Kuestermann, Behn Meyer, Shiffman Heer and Paterson Simon which handled the import-export trade. These shipping offices have extensive warehousing at the back, sometimes with granite-paved alleys going right through them to Lebuh Pantai. Today, they wait to be renovated for more contemporary use on a case by case basis. For example, the **British Council Library** is

Typical day at Lebuh Pantai, Penang's financial district

The British Council premises at Pengkalan Weld

now in the former Behn Meyer office at No.3 Pengkalan Weld which has been attractively refurbished.

The present conservation guidelines safeguard the facades of the turn-of-the-century shipping offices but not the warehouses and the alleyways that run from Pengkalan Weld to Lebuh Pantai. The earlier 19th century buildings of the port do have interesting stories to tell about the history of the port, demonstrating the thousands of coolies who migrated here to eke out a living and required by the labour-intensive machinery used in the days of sailing ships.

Of the water villages along Weld Quay, the **Chew Jetty** located at the end of Gat Lebuh Armenian is the largest and most lively. The jetty of the Chew clan is one of Penang's many "clan jetties", which are actually clan villages built on water. The timber houses are joined by plank walkways. The jetties were set up in the 19th century and the jetty-dwellers worked as stevedores and cross-channel ferry boatmen in the bustling port of Penang. Today, a stand at the end of Chew Jetty offers *sampan* (a small boat with a stern oar or oars) cruises along the waterfront. The Chew jetty is a very attractive tourist attraction for those interested in seeing a community which has remained remarkably unchanged for hundreds of years.

The plank walkways of Chew Jetty are characteristic of water villages

From Chew Jetty, it is a short walk to the **Lebuh Victoria Bus Terminal,** where you can see one of the early 19th century warehouses, belonging to the Khaw family. From here you can get a bus to Komtar, and from there to the rest of the island.

The Chulia Street Scene
Lebuh Chulia, Lorong Love, Lebuh Leith

Budget tourists find cheap hotels, ticketing and cafes; sailors and itinerant salesmen come for the red light district; locals look for rattan shops, hardware stores, frames and furniture; by night, the place is alive with pubs and street hawkers - all this along a street which is rich with Indian Muslim mosques, religious schools and burial grounds. Contrasting values and cultures have co-existed for a long time, making Chulia Street a place of great character and notoriety.

For a large number of tourists, Chulia Street is the most important street in Penang and the centre of a well-established backpacker scene. It all began in the 1960s when the Vietnam War made Bangkok the hub of relatively cheap flights from many parts of the world. In those days, the great Southeast Asian overland adventure consisted of flying to Bangkok, catching a 24-hour train to Penang - with an optional stop at Koh Samui - then continuing by train to Singapore, by boat or plane to Jakarta, overland across Java to Bali, then back again perhaps by bus along the East Coast of Peninsular Malaya from Singapore and finally from Kota Bharu and Golok to Bangkok.

Getting off the ferry in George Town, the backpacker would be greeted by trishaws offering to take them to cheap hotels along Lebuh Chulia (Chulia Street) and, off this road and from east to west, along Jalan Pintal Tali (Rope Walk), Lorong Love (Love Lane), Lebuh Cintra and Lebuh Leith.

These cheap hotels originally catered to lusty sailors and itinerant salesmen, but the backpackers didn't mind, even if they were looking for a different sort of action. Over time, the Chinese inns-cum-brothels were gradually transformed into budget hotels, promoted in international guide books for budget travellers.

Chulia Street's charm today is still best described by the following remark made by an European ex-tourist: "... people [here] were devoted to indulging in life's simple pleasures - going to the cinema,

33

sampling all varieties of hawker food, listening to traditional music and organising joget or ronggeng parties. Walking along Muntri Street then, you could hear the endless clatter of *mahjong* tiles. People were always out on the street, talking to each other and to tourists. They were happy."

Apart from budget hotels and travel agencies, Chulia Street, more recently, has added antique and collectibles shops, Burmese and Chinese crafts shops, second-hand bookstores, and a variety of local and western food cafes, all adding to the street's attractions for the budget visitor. At the same time, traditional activities, such as the cane and rattan craft shops, picture-framing and mirror shops still remain to be patronised by locals.

Cheapside, a small alley off Chulia Street, has a row of hardware stalls with almost every variety of bathroom and carpentry accessory one can wish to look for. For more unusual souvenirs, Lim Tan Tin has a workshop that makes *mahjong* tiles and dice on

Budget hotel converted from Anglo-Indian bungalow on Lebuh Chulia

Elaborate entrance to the forecourt of Teo-chew Association building on Lebuh Chulia

Lorong Love.

At night, the street hawkers take over Lebuh Cintra, Kampung Mala-bar, Lebuh Chulia and the adjoining section of Jalan Penang. This stretch of Jalan Penang is also well known for Chinese restaurants, Japanese hostess lounges and adult nightlife.

Every morning, **Lebuh Carnarvon**, just off Chulia Street, turns into a roadside wet market, selling everything from fish, vegetables and meats to cheap clothes, slippers, crockery and knick-knacks.

Further along this way, you will come to the **Campbell Street Market** which is housed in a turn-of-the-century building. Straight ahead, the shophouses along **Lebuh Carnarvon** specialise in dried and preserved foods. Spice shops here have modernised their business and now produce instant mixes for Penang's favourite hawker foods such as *Laksa* and *Hokkien Mee* for export throughout the world.

Lebuh Chulia

As Cullin and Zehnder wrote of the old town in 1905, "Different parts of the town were assigned to the various nationalities, and the Chulias, natives of India, still

All manner of craft shops, hotels and food outlets can be found in terrace shophouses like this along Lebuh Chulia

occupy the same locality as they did in the good old days". In the early years of George Town, the Indian Muslims, once prominent traders and shippers, owned fabulous compound houses around Lebuh Chulia. But by the end of the 19th century, many of these businesses had lost out to European shipping. The compound houses were sold off, or shophouses were built along the street front, obscuring the original properties. Many of the original Anglo-Indian bungalows around Lebuh Chulia Street have been converted into budget hotels.

An early 19th century bungalow located at the western end of Lebuh Chulia next to the Himayathul Anjuman Islam has a curious history. Most probably built as an Indian Muslim residence, for some years before the First World War, it became the premises of the *Jit-Pun-A Kong*

Kwang or Japanese Club.

At the turn-of-the-century, Penang was well known for Japanese prostitutes known as *karayuki-san*. The Japanese Club building fits the description found in James Low's dissertation of 1836: "A substantial bungalow, from 60-70

feet long by 34-40 broad - the under storey of brick and mortar, the upper constructed with the best kinds of wood, with a tiled roof, and the whole interior and exterior of the upper storey painted - might be built perhaps for some twelve hundred Spanish dollars. .. Some of the richest natives are

Nagore Shrine with built-in arcade at the eastern end of Lebuh Chulia

Entrace to the Noordin family tomb on Lebuh Chulia

beginning to build brick houses." Similar houses which belonged to wealthy Arabs can be found in the Acheen Street Mosque compound on Lebuh Aceh.

Lebuh Chulia is also the milieu for a large collection of Indian Muslim waqf (endowment) lands. From east to west, these are the **Nagore Shrine** (1801), the **Noordin family mausoleum** (before 1870), the Kapitan Keling Mosque (1801), '**Ashrakal**' which is connected to a Muslim cemetery along Jalan Masjid off Chulia Street (from 1840s), the **Dahudi Bohra Mosque** (1910s), the **Masjid Alim Shahwali** (tomb from 1811) and the **Himayathul Anjuman Islam**.

The **Noordin family mausoleum** is located at the northeast corner of the Kapitan Keling Mosque. Mohamed Merican Noordin, alias M.M. Noordin, came to Penang around 1820 and became the most prominent Indian Muslim shipping merchant and philanthropist of his time. He contributed generously towards the cost of laying down pipes from the Waterfall for the town's water supply and was one of the first Muslims to be made a Municipal Commissioner and Justice of the Peace. He built the tomb for his mother, and was himself buried there after 1870.

The tomb's vestibule accommodated a school for the Muslim community endowed "for the learning of English, Hindoostanee, Malay, Tamil, Malabar, and the Alkoran. Twenty dollars a month." Although the Noordins were the wealthiest Muslim family in the latter half of the 19th century, the magnificent mausoleum, through neglect, is now in ruins.

On the whole, Lebuh Chulia is interesting for its lovely streetcape, off-street compounds and alleyways. This area is called "Cultural Precinct '- Chulia Street/Love Lane" under the conservation guidelines, which emphasize streetscape conservation.

Lorong Love, Lorong Stewart, Lebuh Muntri

The residential area around Lorong Stewart, and from Lebuh Muntri to Lebuh Leith, can be approached by any of the streets going north from Lebuh Chulia, or, from the Goddess of Mercy Temple at Jalan Masjid Kapitan Keling.

Along Lorong Stewart, you can drop in at the **Penang Heritage**

Malaya first stayed at the guild premises before proceeding to other parts of the country to work.

Due to modernisation of the building industry, the role and status of carpenters has been greatly diminished. However, these old tradesmen still play a crucial part in the repair and on-going maintenance of our heritage buildings. As many of the workers are wage-labourers, on "no-work" days, they gather here to play mah-jong. Restoration of their building was initiated by the Penang Heritage Trust which contributed to raising funds for the project.

Next to the Carpenters' Guild on Lorong Love is the Shih Chung school, opposite the **Sun Tak Association**. There are more associations belonging to the Cantonese and Hainanese nearby.

From east to west along Lebuh Muntri (which continues from Lebuh Stewart), you will find, to your left, the **Tailors' Association**, the **Surname Association, Leong See Kah Meow**, the **Goldsmith's Guild**, and the **Penang Restaurant and Tea Shops As-**

Entrance to Crapenter's Guild on Lorong Love off Lebuh Chulia

Trust office at 26A. Here you can make inquiries, suggestions, and offer assistance as you wish.

The Trust occupies a turn-of-the-century shophouse which was formerly a Hainanese seafarers' lodge called *Loon Ngee Hing*, literally, "Lodge of the Artisans of the Wheel". Most of the Chinese artisans who came to Penang hailed from Canton, and their associations are concentrated in this neighbourhood. In 1794, Francis Light wrote that "The Chinese residents are the most skilful carpenters, construction workers and machinery workers."

The mid-19th century **Carpenters' Guild**, or *Lo Pan Hang*, in Lorong Love, is the association of Cantonese carpenters and builders whose forefathers constructed many of Penang's heritage buildings, as well as, highly skilled joiners who crafted the Straits Chinese and other "colonial" furniture.

Lo Pan is the patron deity of all Chinese carpenters, and carpentry is first among all the building trades. All builders who came to

Making joss sticks in Lorong Love

Joss sticks drying in the sun in Lorong Love

sociation. The **Goldsmith's Guild** or *Ta Kam Hong*, founded in 1832, is the oldest and largest association of goldsmiths in Malaysia. The present guild temple was erected on Lebuh Muntri in 1903.

On the right of the same road are the former **Lam Wah Ee Hospital** and the **Shaolin Athletic Association**. The latter provides traditional Chinese physiotherapy and also serves as a centre for martial arts training. Quite a number of Western tourists come to learn martial arts here.

The Hainanese were the last of the five major dialect groups (Hokkien, Hakka, Cantonese, Teochew and Hainan) to migrate to Penang. Finding most occupations already monopolised, in the early 20th century, they somehow created a niche for themselves as cooks, coffee-shop owners and hoteliers. The **Hainanese Association**, or *Thean Ho Keong*, on Lebuh Muntri, was founded in 1895. The temple committee decided their temple was too plain and, for their centenary, invited Hokkien craftsmen from China to

decorate it. The result is a visually wondrous Hokkien-style facade, complete with swirling roof decorations and dragon pillars guaranteed to confound future cultural interpreters. Opposite is the Hong Kong shoe store, where you can buy custom-made Nyonya-style headed slippers.

Lebuh Leith

A number of budget hotels are found along Lebuh Leith. The medium-budget Cathay Hotel, housed in a heritage mansion with a lovely inner courtyard, is a favourite among visiting artists and writers. Leith Street has been revitalised, thanks to the restoration of several buildings, including the **Cheong Fatt Tze Mansion** and its servants' quarters opposite which have since been converted for use as eating and drinking places.

The fully restored Cheong Fatt Tze Mansion on Lebuh Leith was privately undertaken using craftsmen from China

Around Komtar
Penang Road, Chinatown shopping, and the Seven Streets Precinct

Penang people eat and shop in Chinatown, and pay their bills at Komtar (Tun Abdul Razak Complex), a major building complex with a sixty-five storey tower built by the state as part of its urban renewal programme. In the vicinity are three wet markets and many small family businesses which characterise Penang's commercial milieu. At the Seven Streets precinct south of Komtar, the working class continue to live in prewar terrace houses.

Komtar is the ultimate landmark from which to orientate yourself in George Town. Sited at the southernmost end of Jalan Penang, this is where the island's primary bus terminal is found. It is bound to the north by Jalan Dr. Lim Chwee Leong (Prangin Road), beyond which is an area designated "Markets & Shopping Precinct - Chinatown". Its southern boundary is Jalan Magazine, which is the first of the seven parallel roads designated the "Seven Streets Precinct" . To the west and east are the southern halves of Jalan Penang and Lebuh Carnarvon, respectively. The Chinatown shopping area is delineated by Lebuh Campbell, Lebuh Kimberley, Jalan Penang and Lebuh Carnarvon.

KOMTAR

The **Kompleks Tun Abdul Razak**, built in stages during the 1970s and 80s, is named after the second Prime Minister of Malaysia. It was designed by the architect Lim Chong Keat, brother of the then Penang Chief Minister. Komtar was intended to be the highrise to end all highrises. At 65 floors, with a helipad on top, it remains the tallest building in Penang. The three tiers of government - Federal, State and Municipal - are all located in the tower.

Komtar is to George Town what the Eiffel Tower is to Paris. For tourists and Penangites, the 58th floor Viewing Gallery is a must, as it offers a superb view of the terracotta roofscapes of the old city. Your RM5 admission ticket here can also be used to purchase souvenirs.

Komtar is the closest thing George Town has to a civic centre. The entrance to all the government offices in the tower is located at the Level Three Concourse. Complaints to the **Municipal Council of Penang Island** can be made here **(MPPP Hotline 604 - 263 7637).**

The urban renewal project around Komtar is still going on after two decades.

Jalan Penang

Stretching in a south-easterly direction, from Lebuh Farquhar in the north to its junction with Jalan Magazine, Jalan Gurdwara (Brick Kiln Road), Jalan Datuk Keramat and Jalan Macalister in the south, Jalan Penang is the westernmost border of the inner city. It remains a good place to shop for photographic equipment, curios and pewter.

Following the one-way road system implemented in 1996, the southern half of Jalan Penang is a one-way street going north, while the northern half is another one-way system moving traffic southwards. The two meet at Jalan Burmah and Jalan Dr. Lim Chwee Leong (Prangin Road), directing traffic flow west and east, respectively.

Five main roads, Jalan Penang, Jalan Magazine, Jalan Gurdwara, Jalan Dato' Keramat and Jalan Macalister, all meet at the KOMTAR junction

The **Penang Tourist Guides' Association** has an Information Centre on the Level Three Concourse which is open from 10am to 6pm - seven days a week - and has the most knowledgeable and helpful advisor in Ms Khoo, for visitors in need of information on Penang's many products and services.

Komtar's four-storey podium houses two department stores, two bookstores, three fast food outlets, two large *batik* shops, two

food courts, three cinemas, as well as opticians, florists, restaurants and a host of shops selling clothes, computers, music, and computer software, watches, without end. The **Malaysian Airline (MAS) reservation and ticketing office** is situated on the ground floor.

Most importantly, Komtar is the public transport hub, hence the local proverb "all buses lead to KOMTAR". It is also a good place to catch a taxi by day or night.

The southern half of Jalan Penang is mostly lined with shops selling clothes, cameras, rattan goods, and souvenir products.

From the Jalan Farquhar end in the north, major rehabilitation and development projects are under way. From the ongoing refurbishment and new construction of the Eastern & Oriental Hotel on Jalan Farquhar, to the renewal of the Wearne Brothers building (owned by the Loke Wan Yat family of

Lebuh Kimberley has all its shophouses and eateries catering to the the Chinese community in Penang

Kuala Lumpur) opposite, and the redevelopment and new building of a row of city hotels offering superb accommodation and comfort to visitors who prefer the convenience of being in the city.

Of the renewal and new building undertaken to provide better accommodation for city visitors, the **City Bayview** (see page 94) now has a spanking new block, just east of Jalan Penang, while the **Cititel Penang** (see page 93) is a completely new hotel built on the land where the Cold Storage Creameries building used to be.

Moving south, you pass the Odeon and Cathay, two of the island's older cinemas, as well as the imposing police headquarters complex. Opposite the police complex is the **Chowrasta wet market** which was rebuilt to provide for a host of dry-goods outlets deemed necessary by locals. The Chowrasta market sells local foodstuffs and the adjacent **Jual Murah** (Cheap Sales) has a plethora of bargain stalls selling textiles and bags. In the morning, Chowrasta Market is the largest and busiest wet market in the inner city. It is also considered one of the cheapest.

Chinatown

Lebuh Kimberley, the road parallel to, and north of **Jalan Dr. Lim Chwee Leong** (Prangin Road), is a popular eating street in the morning and at night. One night stall sells assorted traditional Chinese desserts such as almond soup, peanut soup and glutinous rice porridge. **Goh Huat Seng** is a Teochew steamboat restaurant popular with the locals. Some of the modest looking shops selling joss sticks and other prayer items have made large fortunes. One of them, **Bee Chin Heong**, has even opened a gallery selling art from China and other home decorations for the Chinese nouveau riche. **New Asia Hotel**, at the corner of Lebuh Kimberley and Jalan Pintal Tali, is a cheap, clean budget hotel. Newly built when the Japanese Occupation began, it was first used to lodge Japanese officers and then American GIs just after the war.

Lebuh Campbell, the next road parallel to Lebuh Kimberly, used to be one of the main shopping streets in the city before KOMTAR and the other shopping malls came along. The shops here sell handbags, shoes, clothes and electricals. Other interesting outlets along Lebuh Campbell include Chinese medicine halls, the **Ten-Ren** tea house, dim sum coffee shops and everybody's favourite chicken rice shop, **Thor Yuen** (near the junction with Jalan Pintal Tali). **Taj** and **Hameediyah** are two old Indian Muslim restaurants well known for *murtabak*, which tastes a bit like quiche.

41

In the mid-1980s, the first pedestrianisation plan in Penang was drawn up for Lebuh Campbell by urban designers from Yokohama city. Due to the general lack of recreational space for children living in the inner city, a trial road block at Lebuh Campbell was introduced, creating the unexpected scene of hundreds of children playing in the streets. In those days, none of the shopkeepers wanted traffic-calming, believing that every Penang customer wants to stop his or her car right in front of the shop. However, a generation later, the mood has changed. Now most of the shopkeepers favour pedestrianisation in the belief that it will boost business. Lebuh Campbell is closed to traffic annually during the *Shopping Carnival* in October.

Lebuh Carnarvon, the eastern border of George Town's Chinatown, is well known for Chinese bookshops, art supplies, stationery shops, as well as undertakers. The latter are makers of wooden coffins and of the paper offerings (called *kong teik*), made of coloured paper, tinsel and bamboo, to accompany the dead on their "journey". During funerals and anniversaries, the Chinese present their dead with the material necessities and luxuries which they believe they may need in the next world; mansions and servants, Mercedes Benzes and chauffeurs, clothes, credit cards and "Hell notes" - these expensive paper artefacts simply go up in smoke at the end of the ceremonies.

Lebuh Cintra is named after a port in Portugal, recalling a time when the Eurasians lived here. Now it is locally known as *Jit-Pun Kay*, for this street and the adjoining Kampung Malabar were well

Just completed pedestrianised roadway of Lebuh Cambell

known in the early 20th century as a Japanese red light district, with Japanese camera shops and watch shops in the vicinity. Today, Lebuh Cintra is a popular supper place, selling hot broth, a savoury doughnut-like pastry called *hum-chin-peng* and medicinal teas.

Jalan Pintal Tali was originally called Rope Walk because of the rope-spinning that was done along this street. This activity was carried out by Tamil Muslims and the rope was delivered by bullock-cart drivers to the waterfront where they were used for moor-

Shops along Lebuh Carnarvon which produce and sell Chinese funeral paper products

ing the ships. The bullock-cart drivers subsequently moved their base to Jalan Dr. Lim Chwee Leong, where they would park their wooden carts along the Prangin canal. There is a local saying for the miserly Penangite, that his "one cent is as big as a bullock cart wheel".

In the Chinatown area, you will find many stalls with the sign "Economy Food" or "Economy Rice". What it really means is cheap food, usually rice served with a number of side dishes of your choice. The cooking at all these stalls is quite similar to Pen-

The brightly painted Diamond Jubilee Sikh Temple on Jalan Gurdwara (previously, Jalan Brick Kiln)

ang Chinese home cooking.

The **Month of the Hungry Ghosts** (August - September) is celebrated by many market, hawker and Chinese residents' associations all over George Town. Chinese opera, Canton pop performances and "drive-in" cinemas are put up in the middle of the road, together with instant altars to a giant paper effigy of the King of the Hungry Ghosts, whose duty it is to round up all the ghosts at the end of the month and put them back into (the) Hades. Penang is the only place in the country where this festival is celebrated on such an extensive scale.

Seven Streets Precinct

The "Seven Streets Precinct" south of Komtar is a relatively new name referring to the triangle-shaped area bounded by Jalan Magazine, Lebuh Cecil, Lebuh C.Y. Choy (Bridge Street), and

Jalan Gudwara (Brick Kiln Road), to the north, south, east and west, respectively. Although it is the building and communal ambience of the east-west roads for which the area was selected by the Municipal Council's Design Guidelines for Conservation, there is also a turn-of-the-century Sikh temple on Jalan Gurdwara to be found here.

The local Hokkien-speaking population refer to the east-west streets in this area by their sequence from the Prangin canal (presently, by Komtar) - Jalan Magazine, Lebuh Noordin, Lebuh Presgrave, Lebuh Tye Sin, Lebuh Macallum, Lebuh Katz and Lebuh Cecil are called the Hokkien equivalent of "street number one", "street number two" and so on. Although there are more than seven parallel streets, the popularity of the *chit-tiau law bansan* (or the "street number seven" municipal market) at Cecil Street, makes this generic area name

resonant.

While several blocks within the Seven Streets Precinct area do date from the turn of the century, the bulk of this "inner suburbia" consists of row upon row of double-storey residential terraced houses dating from the 1920s and 1930s. A stylised "Straits eclectic shophouse" is basically a terraced house with a highly decorated facade - with stuccoed motifs, carved wooden doors, batshaped vents above the windows and glazed and embossed dado tiles below. Traditional terraced houses are generically called "shophouses" even though they may be designed and used exclusively as residences.

Although the original residents and perhaps even the present landlords of these rent control houses may be Straits Chinese, the Seven Streets Precinct has for some time been a solid working-class Hokkien neighbourhood.

These terrace houses along Jalan McNair with moulded columns and wooden slatted windows are typical of the buildings found throughout the "Seven Streets Precinct".

The residential character of these terraced houses still predominates. However, many commercial activities such as vehicle repair workshops have crept in. Some of the houses have charming forecourts which were probably once neat little gardens but have now been cemented over for use as car-parks.

The area is also well-known for the spirit-medium cult temples which organise the nine-day *Nine Emperor God festivals* during the ninth lunar month every year (around October). As part of the festival, the spirit-mediums, dressed in royal yellow, perform pain-defying feats such as bowling with red hot iron balls, drinking boiling oil, spearing their cheeks with long lances and other forms of self-flagellation. This festival is held simultaneously in a number of Chinese urban areas in Malaysia, but it is the spirit-medium of Phuket, south Thailand,

who have a reputation for taking it to the most gory extremes. The Phuket and Penang traditions are historically related.

The Zones

A note about the "zones": the Seven Streets Precinct appeared as Zone I under the Municipal Council's "Design Guidelines for Conservation Areas in the Inner city of George Town, Penang" of 1987. To illustrate the nature of these guidelines, about one-third of George Town's inner city was zoned for redevelopment along the lines of the Grand Continental Hotel, another one-third for redevelopment to about five-storeys and a little less than one-third to be conserved. The guidelines are currently being revised for incorporation into the Local Plan by Penang's Heritage Unit. **The Heritage Centre** in Penang is located at **128 Lebuh Armenian**.

From **Shangri-La Hotel** and KOMTAR, you can head out to the middle suburbs via Jalan Dato' Keramat and Jalan Macalister.

The new towering **UMNO Building** on Jalan Macalister was designed by environmental architecture proponent, Ken Yeang, and is planned as an environmental building design.

Down Jalan Zainal Abidin, formerly called Yahudi Road, is the **Jewish cemetery**, which holds over a hundred graves in a large, rectangular enclosed round. The Jews who came to Penang after World War I were mostly poor pedlars. During World War II, the community evacuated to Singapore and few ever came back. There used to be a Jewish Synagogue at a 1920s corner shophouse at 28 Jalan Nagore, but no longer.

North Beach and the North Coast Suburbs

Millionaire's Row, Gurney Drive, Pulau Tikus

Highrise offices now stalk George Town's Millionaire's Row. The plush suburb by the sea, once lined with fabulous mansions, tells the story of rags to riches, and of riches to ruins. The low-rise suburbs of Pulau Tikus, historically a home for Penang's Eurasian, Thai, Burmese and Arab minorities, is now a hub for pubs and restaurants. The Gurney Drive esplanade is popular for recreational walks and hawker food.

The tree-lined avenue of Jalan Sultan Ahmad Shah (Northam Road) used to be the Millionaires' Row of Penang. It was originally an European suburb along the north beach. However, by the turn-of-the-century, the Chinese millionaires were beginning to take over, vying with each other to see who could build the most fabulous and fanciful mansion.

Jalan Sultan Ahmad Shah

You can take a trishaw from Gurney Drive into town via Jalan Sultan Ahmad Shah i.e. from west to east. Not the other way, as half of this grand avenue is now a one-way street. On your ride, you will see old and new Penang standing in stark contrast on either side of the road. Beginning from the western end of Jalan Sultan Ahmad Shah, the first mansion on your right is **Hardwicke**, dwarfed by a huge highrise under construction. The next three or four buildings on your right are also high-density towers.

The surviving heritage mansions are on the left, to the seaward side of the road. The first mansion is the residence of a Teochew planter, distinguished by its green domed tower, dating from 1925 and named **Woodville**. After this comes a large gray building faced with Shanghai plaster. This is the **Istana Kedah**, the Kedah royal family's residence in Penang. And next to this is **Homestead**. It was commissioned in 1919 by a shipping magnate, Lim Mah Chye, who went bankrupt several years later and sold it to Yeap Chor Ee, founder of

Stained glass windows of the Leong Yin Kean Mansion

Unlike neighbouring houses , Woodville remains in good condition (Jalan Sultan Ahmad Shah)

Ban Hin Lee Bank, whose descendants still live in this house and keep it furnished with antiques. All three early 20th century mansions were designed by European architects or civil engineers.

Further on lies a small dirt lane turning towards the beach. This leads to **The Aloes**, one of the original European bungalows by the sea, dating from the mid-19th century and now occupied by a CD store. The next turning to the beach will take you to **Paramount Hotel** with a seafood restaurant in an annexe built to house it. Beyond this is a "butterfly" bungalow (with the left and right wings of the building angled forward instead of extending at right angles from the middle portion of the structure) now abandoned; **Soonstead**, also abandoned; and then a new highrise hotel which is being built on the site of the Metropole Hotel, which was illegally demolished on Christmas Day several years ago. The large military camp after the Citibank Wisma Penang Garden building was formerly the Runnymede Hotel, a premier place to stay before the war, ri-

valled only by the E & O Hotel.

Then we come to the house of the late Loh Boon Siew, a multi-millionaire who rose from rags to riches through real estate and the Honda franchise. Admired for his "needless" thrift as well as his philanthropy, he became an antique collector towards the end of his life and took apart the gilded doors and ironwork from his other heritage properties to embellish his Art Deco home. Following this is a fenced up empty site where another mansion, Brook Lodge, was illegally demolished on Chinese New Year's day in 1989. The ground here still has one of the best specimens of *Lagerstroemia Loundonii* which blossoms during the dry season, around the anniversary of the illegal demolition.

Almost opposite this building, on the other side of the road, is a large three-storey mansion known as **Shih Chung School**, of unique Anglo-Chinese architecture. It was formerly called the Chinese Residency, and at one time served as the Bellevue hotel, then as the Raffles-by-the-sea hotel, before it was used as a school

and subsequently abandoned.

The last bungalow of note and on the beach side of the road is the **Leong Yin Kean Mansion**, designed by Charles Miller in 1926. This beautiful "Garden House", with floral mosaic on its floor and facade, Italian marble, stained glass windows and a teak stairway that is still in good condition, was built for a quarter of a million Straits Dollars. Now under corporate ownership represented by businessman Datuk Nazir Arif, it is being restored, at an estimated cost of half a million Ringgit, for use as his group of companies' headquarters, with a private art gallery and theme restaurant planned to occupy the more public areas of the building.

Many of Penang's old mansions are abandoned because the original families are no longer interested in the upkeep of an older and more expensive style of living. The saying goes that the Straits Chinese cannot keep their wealth beyond three generations: the first generation makes it, the second consolidates, and the third fritters it away; then the descend-

Highrise buildings line Jalan Sultan Ahmad Shah

 ing facilities and rubbish disposal. Some favourite foods here are *laksa, ais kachang,* soya bean milk and *rojak.* The section for halal Muslim food, offers *satay, pasembur, mee bandung* and other rice and noodle dishes.

The large white building near the western end is **Uplands School**, a UK-curriculum international school for expatriate children housed in the former St. Joseph's Novitiate building. The "butterfly villa" next to it is an Arts and Crafts - style seaside mansion built by a descendant of the wealthy tin-mining Loke family in Kuala Lumpur.

ants squabble over the family estate and sell their ancestral homes to the highest bidder. Despite the fate of the families, however, the buildings remain as a symbol of a time gone by when the "haves" really had it all.

Almost directly opposite the demolished Metropole Hotel site is Jalan Larut. At the road's curve to the right is another heritage mansion called **Limburg**, which has been an outlet (equipped with a children's playground) for a franchise fast food outlet for some years now.

Gurney Drive

Persiaran Gurney, continuing west along the north coastline, and still popularly called Gurney Drive, used to be lined with seaside bungalows and casuarina trees. Some of these bungalows have been converted to seaside cafes, while others have been replaced by sea-facing hotels, like the **Evergreen Laurel Hotel** (see page 96), as well as condominium and hybrid commercial developments.

Still the most popular esplanade in Penang, the 2-kilometre Gur-

ney Drive is where many come early for their morning walks, *tai-chi* and herbal pork rib soup (*bah kut teh*), families come in the evenings, bringing their out-of-town guests, and young bikers race along the road after midnight.

At the western end of Gurney Drive is the municipal hawker centre, popular among locals and tourists alike, with a great variety of stalls. The hawkers used to line the esplanade but were moved to one centralised location for the purpose of providing better wash-

Recently, the number of highrise condominiums erected have cut off, for many, the view and breeze of the sea they previously enjoyed. With plans already made to reclaim the waterfront 0.8 kilometres out to the sea, the condominium owners, now enjoying their sea views, may suffer the same problems their buildings have caused to those before them!

Although Gurney Drive is not regarded as a sacred place, three important festivals are associated

Persiaran Gurney's arts and crafts-style "butterfly" villa is next to the former St Joseph's Novitiate which now houses the Uplands UK-curriculum international school at the western end of the road

with this esplanade. The first was the ***Dragon Boat Race***, held on the fifth day of the fifth lunar month, which has since been relocated to the Mengkuang Dam (see page 74) on the mainland. The second is the Thai water festival, ***Loy Krathong***, held late in the year. This starts with a small procession around the Thai temples and ends with paper boats and flowers, with lighted candles, being cast adrift in the sea. The third is the ***Nine Emperor Gods festival*** which begins with a long procession from Lebuh Carnarvon and ends in Gurney Drive, where the spirit-mediums send a miniature ship out to sea.

Pulau Tikus

Pulau Tikus (literally, "Rat Isle"), is a tiny island situated just north of Penang Island. However, when people talk of Pulau Tikus they are usually referring to a middle-class suburb of George Town.

The main street and centre of Pulau Tikus is Jalan Burma, where it makes a junction with Jalan Cantonment.

Pulau Tikus has been home to several historic communities, namely Eurasians, Burmese, Siamese, Arabs and Straits Chinese. Today, it is a choice address for the Penang middle-class and expatriates. The suburb has maintained its roadside trees and low building density. The single exception is the very dense shopping centre called **Midlands Complex**, or alternatively, the **One-Stop Centre**, where many cheap computer CD stores can be found.

Pulau Tikus is growing to be like Singapore's Holland Park Village. It has become a favourite place to wine and dine, with a wide choice of pubs and specialised

eating outlets. There is an extensive mix of German, Italian, Japanese, Chinese and boutique restaurants, together with coffee bars and local coffee shops which offer nearly all of Penang's hawker foods, all within walking distance from one other in this small suburb. The small community's two rows of old and new shoplots also house banks, furniture stores, and a full range of household goods and services outlets. **The Art Gallery** (see page 108) at **Bellisa Row** (which is a good example Penang terrace shoplots to come) regularly organises current art exhibitions and has a file on most of Penang's contemporary artists.

Going south from the Jalan Burma-Jalan Cantonment cross junction takes you past a small shopping complex to the right, and the **Pulau Tikus Market** to your left. This market is often called the "rich wives' wet market" as you

The busy Pulau Tikus traffic junction on a typical day shows the attraction this suburb has for many Penangites

The Wat Chaiya Mangkalaram on Lorong Burma

can buy the more expensive varieties of fish and *kampong* chicken (non-battery chicken) here. In the mornings, one of the small stalls around the market sells a remarkable variety of Nyonya dishes such as *nasi ulam* (herbal rice) and *kerabu beehoon* (spiced vermicelli salad). A hawker complex springs up in front of the market in the late evening.

The turn on the right, just past the market from Jalan Cantonment, is Jalan Moulmein. The first terrace house on this road is **Clay Craft** (see page 109) a shop selling its own range of pottery products, furniture, clothes, gift items and household accessories. Set up by its architect-theologian proprietor, Tim Yee, this outlet has become popular among locals and the expatriate community for the originality of its product designs and reasonable prices.

Following Britain's takeover of the

island, Pulau Tikus became the site of a Burmese village. Fishermen and cultivators once lived here, but all that remains today is the **Dhammikarama Burmese Buddhist temple**, founded in 1805, on Lorong Burma. The stupa and Sima Hall, featured in several early paintings by artists as yet unknown, are worth a visit for examples of temple structures at the turn of the 18th century.

Opposite this temple complex, **Wat Chaiya Mangkalaram**, is a Siamese temple which was officially given its site in 1845. Its 33-metre gold-plated reclining Buddha, once regarded as the third largest in the world, has probably been superceded by more ambitious new statues. Photography is prohibited unless you commission the temple photographer to do so.

Throughout their history, both temples have been mainly supported by wealthy women patrons.

As a result of their generous donations, more and more fanciful structures have been put up in recent years. The traditional Buddhist festival of *Sonkran* (around the month of April) is a joyous occasion which gives people an excuse to behave like children and splash water on each other. The water splashing begins at the Thai temple and moves on to the Dhammikarama.

Pulau Tikus was in its prime during the internecine period, when the Straits Chinese and Eurasians [Siamese] led a charmed existence amidst their holiday bungalows, fruit orchards and horse stables. All over Pulau Tikus there are pretty bungalows raised on brick piers, with a space just big enough to crawl under. At the junction of Jalan Kelawai and facing Jalan Cantonment, a classical Penang bungalow, dated 1918 on its facade, was built by a Jew named D'Mordicai and recently

The Church of Immaculate Conception was and remains a focal point of the Eurasian community which relocated from Phuket in 1810.

history, the land was originally meant for the Catholic poor, although the Church held the title to it. The Church has since developed this "under-utilised" land in a joint-venture operation to build a number of apartment blocks.

In 1992, the assortment of timber homes at Kampung Serani were cleared away, not without resistance from those who were still being housed there, as well as from the Eurasians and people in the community. The Eurasians in the end compromised in favour of a "Heritage House", a community centre provided by the developer.

Also along Jalan Burma lies an Arab village called **Kampung Syed**. Nearby is **Pak Kechik's**, an assortment of roadside food stalls at the junction of Jalan Jones and Jalan Kelawei, which has grown to become the social centre of the Malay community in Pulau Tikus. Whether you have Pak Kechik's early morning *nasi lemak*, the famous Jones Road curry puffs or Malay cakes for afternoon tea, don't miss out on Mat's irresistible *teh tarik* (tea sweetened with condensed milk and "pulled").

restored by Soo Joo Heng of J.Heng Consulting Services.

Catholic community.

Lorong Bangkok is elegantly lined with forty link houses, developed by an early motorcar dealer, Cheah Leong Kah, and designed by Chew Eng Eam, a much-favoured architect of the more affluent Straits Chinese. The street is even prettier at night when the house lights are turned on and scintillate through their coloured glass panes. The architecture is a successful example of link housing, with a parking space for each of the emerging one-car middle-class home of the time, all within a compact neighbourhood rather than in a space-wasteful suburban sprawl.

In 1810, a group of Portuguese Eurasians relocated from Phuket and settled in Pulau Tikus. The **Church of Immaculate Conception** was the focal point of this

Next to the church was the Eurasian village of **Kampung Serani**, which, more than at any other location in Penang, gave the Eurasians a sense of place, belonging, and identity. According to oral

Lorong Bangkok is one of the most successful examples of an integrated neighbourhood planned in the early 20th century

The Green Interior
Jalan Burma, Jalan Macalister, Jalan Dato' Keramat, Penang Botanic Gardens, the Hill Station Township of Air Itam and Penang Hill

Penang's natural heritage of tropical rainforest and great biodiversity, cultural landscape with hills and riverside temples can be found at the Penang Botanic Gardens - the oldest in Malaysia - sited in a beautifully landscaped valley, and the Penang Hills, the oldest British hill station in the tropics.

Three arterial roads take you to the island's green interior. There is Jalan Burma, which links Jalan Penang in the city centre to Jalan Gottlieb and Jalan Mount Erskine in the west; Jalan Macalister, which leads from the Komtar traffic light junction to the Penang Botanic Gardens; and Jalan Dato' Keramat, which begins at the same Komtar junction to Jalan Air Itam (after the Jalan Perak traffic light junction) and the Penang Hill funicular railway station.

Jalan Burma

Running parallel to Jalan Sultan Ahmad Shah, Jalan Burma is also a one-way road from east to west, from Jalan Penang to the Jalan Pangkor traffic light junction.

Up to the Jalan Larut/Jalan Anson traffic light junction, Jalan Burma is lined with residential, commercial, and retail shophouses.

At the abovementioned light junction, **Jalan Anson** (the left turning) is where the Penang branch of **Kolej Damansara Utama** (or, KDU Penang) is located. KDU Penang (see page 104) is certainly one of Penang's more successful private institutions of higher education, with many students from the Indonesia-Malaysia-Thailand Growth Triangle. Part of this college's extensive facilities include an open cyber station where anyone can access the internet for information and for mail. This facility has become very popular among Penang students, which pleases the college authorities no end, as the sta-

KDU Penang's open cyber station within the college premises on Anson Road

The Penang Buddhist Association building on Jalan Anson is perhaps the best example of Straits Chinese ecelectic architecture

tion was set up as part of its computer school's programme to promote IT awareness in Penang.

Towards the Jalan Perak end of Jalan Anson, you will see a building that looks like a beautifully iced birthday cake. This is the **Penang Buddhist Association** on Jalan Anson, perhaps the best example of Straits Chinese ecelectic architecture applied to a temple. The interior includes cast iron staircases, extravagant chandeliers, large mother-of-pearl inlaid blackwood altar tables, lotus-flower patterned floor tiles and a huge altar of *trompe-l'oeil* marble. On **Wesak Day** (around May), hundreds of Buddhist devotees dressed in white assemble here for an evening procession.

Back on Jalan Burma, and continuing straight ahead from the Jalan Anson light junction, many residential quarters were built (just off and along Jalan Burma and all the way west to the Jalan Pangkor traffic light junction) to house the growing number of civil servants in the colonial administration. Many of these are now refurbished for commercial use by the Penang Development Corpo-

ration.

To continue along this road from the Jalan Pangkor light junction, you have to take a left at Jalan Pangkor followed by a right at Jalan Perak, as Jalan Burma is a one-way in the opposite direction(!) from the Jalan Pangkor junction to the Jalan Perak turn-off just ahead.

From Jalan Perak, a left turn will return you to Jalan Burma, where the road continues westward, past several new developments, to Pulau Tikus and the Jalan Gottlieb light junction. A left at this junction will lead to the Jalan Utama (Western Road)/Jalan Waterfall juntion where a right at the small roundabout there is the road to the Penang Botanic Gardens.

Jalan Macalister

Beginning at the Komtar traffic light junction, Jalan Macalister runs from the southern end of Jalan Penang, westward to **Jalan Utama** (Western Road) and the **Penang Botanic Gardens**.

This is another road where many bungalow mansions were built by

the colonial Municipal Council and those who had become rich as Penang grew in prosperity as a free port and trading and commercial centre. The official residence of Penang's Chief Minister is located here.

As in Jalan Sultan Ahmad Shah, many of these mansions have been torn down to make way for impressive office blocks and condominium developments. Most of such changes, however, are near the eastern end of the road. As one moves west, many of the original buildings remain.

The newest change on Jalan Macalister is the **Island Hospital** building (see page 106) and the Moral Uplifting Society building being completed where the residence of a Penang millionaire, Heah Joo Seang, used to be.

To go from town to the Botanic Gardens via Jalan Macalister, a left at the Jalan Anson light junction, followed by a right into Jalan Perak, a left back into Jalan Macalister, another left into Jalan Residensi, a right into Jalan Sepoy Lines, and another right into Jalan Utama is required. This roundabout route replacing the direct Jalan Macalister/Jalan Utama connection is another result of Penang's new one-way road system.

Jalan Dato' Keramat

Jalan Dato' Keramat was the early road to the interior. For travellers in those days, there were two reasons to take this road. The first was to reach the Penang Botanic Gardens (or, Waterfall gardens, as it was then known), an oasis of cool waters in lush tropical jungle for the early settlers. And the second, to get to the heights of Penang Hill for said settlers to escape the tropical heat. The actual road to access both places is Jalan Air Itam which begins where Jalan Dato' Keramat ends, just after the Gaol.

The annual *Thaipusam* procession to the Gardens (late January or early February) also takes this route, and many people follow by foot. Otherwise, the journey today is best made by bicycle or car, as public transport to the Botanic Gardens takes a slightly different route.

According to oral tradition, the village of Dato' Keramat is named after a Tamil Muslim ascetic who founded a settlement of around 1,700, which grew to about 2,000 souls. Later it was apparently sacked by the Sultan of Kedah because it was a hideout for pirates, so by the time the British arrived it was much depopulated.

At the junction of Jalan Dato' Keramat and Jalan Perak is a playing field known as **Padang Brown**. The hawker centre here is well known for *poh piah* (a savoury vegetable roll reminiscent of Vietnamese cooking), *ais kacang* (beans with ice flake topping and rose syrup) and *yong tau*

Fully restored, P.Ramlee's house is just next to the Komplexs Pustaka Warisan Seni

foo (steamboat with an assortment of meatballs and vegetables).

If you turn left from Jalan Dato' Keramat into Jalan Perak, you can follow the signs to the **P. Ramlee House**. The best-loved Malay movie star of all time, P. Ramlee, was a Penangite of Achehnese descent. He was an actor, director, singer, composer and arranger. His black-and-white films, dramas, tragedies and comedies created the "golden age" of Malay cinema. Although he was based in Singapore for the most productive part of his career, P. Ramlee's songs and movies bear the nuances of colloquial Penang Malay and the influences of Penang *Bangsawan* (a "modern" eclectic theatre form).

P. Ramlee's house was in such disrepair by the time conservation work started that it had to be practically rebuilt. The displays at the exhibition house are nicely captioned by the National Archives. Standing in contrast to the modest scale of R. Ramlee's house and the surrounding village homes, is the brand new performing arts complex called

Kompleks Pustaka Warisan Seni, with a theatre seating for up to 300. It is also the office of the state branch of the Ministry of Culture, Arts and Tourism. You can telephone 60 (04) 281 7791 to find out about upcoming performances, and you can also commission a staging of traditional Penang performing arts from here.

On the other side of the P. Ramlee House lies a neatly maintained old Japanese cemetery.

Back to Jalan Dato' Keramat from these places, the turn to your left (at the pedestrian light after Jalan Perak) leads to the **Lorong Kulit Flea Market**. Items sold here range from old photographs, telephone cards and curios to real junk such as second-hand shoes. Browsing and bargaining in this flea market can be a jarring experience, but it won't be boring!

To the Penang Botanic Gardens

Past the stolid wall of the Gaol or state prison on the right of the road, Jalan Dato' Keramat continues as Jalan Air Itam.

To get to the Penang Botanic Gardens from this road, Penang's

The Ayira Vaisya Sri Meenakshi Sundaresvara Temple is just one of three elaborately distinct temples along Jalan Waterfall

new one-way system takes you on another magical mystery tour where you turn right, after you pass the wall of the Penang Gaol, to Jalan Hospital. There, you take another right followed by an immediate left into Jalan Gaol from where you have to take another right into Jalan Lim Khoon Huat to get to Jalan Perak. At Jalan Perak, the road leads to its junction with Jalan Macalister from where you have to opt for the left turn to follow the Jalan Macalister route to the Botanic Gardens.

Another way to the Botanics from Jalan Dato' Keramat is via a right into Jalan York (at the light junction after the one at Jalan Perak), followed by another right into Jalan Scotland (at another light junction), to get on to Jalan Utama and Jalan Waterfall.

The Jalan Sepoy Lines component of the Jalan Macalister route borders a large playing field called the **Polo Ground** where polo is still played.

Around this former parade ground are the **General Hospital**, the **Penang Sports Club**, the **Heritage Club**, and the **Residency**.

Designed by military engineers in 1890, the former governor's Residency, now called *Seri Mutiara*, is the official residence of Penang's Head of State.

The **Penang Caring Society Complex**, located next to the Governor's Residency, is one of the more successful projects undertaken by the Penang State Government in recent times. The complex houses several dozen health and welfare non-governmental organisations under one roof. The **Malaysian Nature Society** is also based here.

The neighbouring building on Jalan Scotland is the **Penang Children's Library**, housed in a renovated old bungalow, behind which flows a lovely clear stream.

Further west, along Jalan Utama (and, after the Jalan Brook/Jalan Macalister light junction), the newly repainted building opposite the Western Road Cemetery is the **Masonic Lodge**. Many of the Europeans in the East were of the Freemasons Lodge; before the war there were several masonic bodies, namely the Lodge Royal Prince of Wales, the Victoria Ju-

bilee Chapter, the Gottlieb Mark Lodge, the Lodge Scotia and the Scotia Chapter. Due to the secrecy that shrouds the masonic lodges all over the country, the local people popularly called the lodge "*Rumah Hantu*" or "Haunted House". The road directly opposite the Masonic Lodge leads to **Youth Park**, a garden gym where crowds gather each evening to jog, exercise, and picnic.

Past Jalan Utama's junction with Jalan Gottlieb, you will come to **Jalan Waterfall** with three major Hindu temples at the foothills by the stream. The oldest one here is the **Nattukottai Chettiar Temple** which dates from the 1850s. The *Thaipusam* silver chariot travels to it via Lorong Kulit, Jalan Air Itam, Jalan Hospital and Jalan Utama.

Opposite the Nattukottai Chettiar Temple is a newly rebuilt temple belonging to the group of chettiars who control the scrap metal and recycling trade. Further along on the left side of the road is a gateway to the **Waterfall Hilltop Temple**, the destination of the *Thaipusam kavadi* procession, in which devotees pierce their persons with long lances and carry large colourful yokes in fulfilment of their vows.

Penang Botanic Gardens

The Penang Botanic Gardens was established by an Englishman, Charles Curtis, in 1884. Curtis was the architect and designer of the gardens, which involved massive landscaping which has remained relatively unchanged since his time. He replanted the former granite quarry and introduced new plants. Originally intended as "a nursery for the planting of colonial products", economic and horticultural plants were brought in from Kew Gardens in England via the Singapore Botanic Gardens.

Also called Waterfall Gardens, the gardens' original attraction was the Waterfall which cascades from a height of over 400 feet. This was once an important source of water supply to the town folk of Penang. At one point Charles Curtis returned to England in despair, for the water authorities were considering turning the entire Botanic Gardens into a reservoir. Fortunately, this plan was not implemented, though a small reservoir was eventually built at the foot of the Waterfall. To view the Waterfall, permission has to be obtained from the Penang Water Authority during office hours.

Located in an "amphitheatre of hills" in the Penang Botanic Gardens, is a natural aboretum. This makes a good hiding place and it became a naval store, ammunition dump and torpedo-assembly station during the Japanese Occupation.

The 72-acre gardens is well loved for their peace and beauty and well used by joggers and walkers. The path around the Lily Pond, only a leisurely ten-minute stroll from the entrance, offers what is probably the most accessible tropical rainforest in Penang.

The walk from the Gardens' Lower Circular Road takes about fifteen minutes and goes past two prominent groups of palms and bamboo clusters along the Waterfall River. Two orchid houses provide comparison between cultivated hybrids and wild orchid species. The best time to admire the flowering trees is during the dry season, from February to April, when the Thai Bungor (L*agestroemia Loudonii*), the Japanese Cassia

The entrance to the Penang Botanic Gardens leads to a 72-acre expanse of greenery and tropical plants from all over the world

(*Cassia javanica*) and the Rosy Trumpet (*Tabebuia rosea*) burst into glorious sprays of colour.

Probably the best collection of plants is at the Fern House. An old employee, Mohd. Ansari, helped to introduce quite a few species of monkey cups and ferns here.

From the Lily Pond path a ten-minute climb will take you to the site of what was formerly Charles Curtis' house, except that only a few bricks now remain. A walk

along the Upper Circular road takes an additional ten minutes. From here you can take a detour to explore the fern rockery, a little forested path by the river.

Various hiking paths lead from the Botanic Gardens to Penang Hill and to Mount Olivia to the north. Mount Olivia was the site of the Raffles' home and was named after Raffles' wife, Olivia, who had a romantic relationship based on a mutual love of literature, with Raffles' best friend, Leyden, following his visit to their house in

Part of the landscaped portion of the Penang Botanic Gardens

Penang.

To Air Itam

From Jalan York, a charming old road which once led to a Scotsman's estate, you can go to **Suffolk House.** The sign "Linear Park" or "*Taman Jajai*" marks the way to the banks of the Air Itam River and Suffolk House just across the bridge.

Back on Jalan Air Itam, and on crossing the river, look out for some laundry hanging by the riverside. **Dhoby Ghaut** is a village of launderers, with Penang's oldest Hindu temple dating from the early 1800s located next to the river.

The **State Mosque**, at the Jalan Air Itam and Jalan Masjid Negeri (Green Lane)/Jalan Scotland intersection, is a landmark with golden onion-shaped domes, and was designed by a Filipino architect. The mosque can accommodate 5,000 worshippers, but as it is not located in the midst of a large Muslim community, it serves more as a "drive-in" mosque on Fridays.

Following the road from here will lead to a small traffic circus where the roads to the farming township of Air Itam, the Penang Hill funicular rail station, and a small housing estate may be accessed respectively.

The Air Itam valley, a fertile stretch of land with a concentration of market gardens at the foot hills make Air Itam's market one of the best places to go for fresh locally-grown vegetables and flowers from Penang Hill. However, much of the farmland has now been turned into housing developments to meet the need for more homes in this growing district.

After getting past the bottleneck

The rolling grounds of the Penang Botanic Gardens

to be found most days at the Air Itam Market, you enter **Paya Terubong Valley**, now a very densely populated housing area indeed. The hill slopes are seen by some to be overdeveloped making them vulnerable to flash flooding and hill slope collapse.

Continuing on to Jalan Relau, you may go to Balik Pulau from the Paya Terubong road. You may also ask around for directions to the **Chung Thye Pin Villa**, which has an abandoned freshwater swimming pool resort built by a tin-mining tycoon around 1930, just off this main road.

The **Kek Lok Si** and a weathered giant statue of the Goddess of Mercy in Air Itam overlooks the Air Itam valley. The Kek Lok Si or the "Temple of Supreme Bliss" as it is often called, with its entrance located just after the town's market, is the country's largest temple complex and was at one time "the only example to be found outside Tibet and mid-China". It has been a popular tourist attraction since the prewar days.

The bulk of the historical complex was constructed between 1893

and 1905. Kek Lok Si was established as a branch of the Buddhist Vatican in the Fujian province of China. Mooted by the chief monk of the Goddess of Mercy Temple, the massive fund-raising and construction project received the solid support of the Straits Chinese elite of Penang.

The Kek Lok Si is geomantically positioned in the "eye of the crane", the crane being the green hills of Ayer Itam. The original complex consisted of a series of monasteries, prayer halls and landscaped gardens. Large boulders set in the hill were inscribed with Chinese verses by famous poets and calligraphers, some of which of these can still be seen in the central courtyard. Today, many of the monastery and prayer hall buildings have been extensively refurbished, complete with airconditioning(!), for the present-day needs of the temple staff.

The growing popularity of Kek Lok Si has led to modern renovations which some might consider excessive. A large new temple building, erected with concrete beams and columns and painted in the style of northern Chinese archi-

The Kek Lok Si, Penang's original Buddhist theme park, on a festival night

tecture, features a large prayer hall upstairs and a den of souvenir shops and vegetarian restaurants downstairs.

Originally built in harmony with the natural landscape, almost every inch of the tiered gardens have now been covered with concrete. Symptomatic of this is the "Liberation Pond", at the top of an old arcade of souvenir shops which flank the steps to the Kek Lok Si, where Buddhists come to "liberate" turtles into an over crowded cemented pond.

The star attraction of the Kek Lok Si, however, is the **Pagoda of Rama VI** which was completed only in 1930. You can make a spiral ascent up this "Pagoda of Ten Thousand Buddhas", which displays "a very fine collection of Alabaster and Bronze Bhuddas". The pagoda building has a Chinese octagonal base, with middle tiers of Thai architecture, and is topped with a Burmese temple crown.

Just uphill from the Kek Lok Si temple is the Air Itam dam, located in the middle of forested hills. The slightly cooler temperature here makes for a pleasant walk or jog along the road around the dam and the resting spot offers a good view of the city below. From the dam it is possible to hike down to Air itam through fruit orchards (less than an hour), up to Tiger Hill (about 1 hour), or to Titi Kerawang, Sungai Pinang, on the other side of the island (several hours).

Penang Hill

The road to the Penang Hill funicular rail station from the Air Itam traffic circus ends at the beginning of the funicular train ride. From here, at the Lower Station, you can ride all the way to the top of Penang Hill in about half an hour.

It was in the hills of Penang where the first hill station in the British Empire was established, shortly after 1800, and even before the famous hill stations of India were considered. The "Convalescent" bungalow at Penang Hill was a place to recuperate from fevers and escape from tropical miasmas. The Europeans were fond of building their second homes here owing to the hills' fresher climate, with temperatures about 3 de-

grees cooler than in George Town.

In the old days, the trip up Penang Hill was made by foot, horse, Achenese pony, or by palanquins or "doolies" carried by Tamil coolies. Today, there is only the funicular railway for visitors to make the trip with.

The hill railway project was eventually taken over by the Penang Municipal Council, only after several private attempts had failed, at the turn of the century. The Governor who launched the services in 1924 declared that "....it is one of the finest Hill Railway in the world today and it is to be hoped that Penang has now become the recognized "Sanitarium" of the Far East. The four original wooden carriages and the present red-and-white cable cars were all made in Switzerland. When first built, the funicular railway system represented a considerable engineering feat for Southeast Asia, and the railway passes through the steepest tunnel in the world. So far, no other challenge to this claim has been made.

The ride from the Lower Station in Ayer Itam to the cool brisk air of Strawberry Hill only takes 30 minutes. The view from Penang Hill is breathtaking. John Turnbull Thomson reminisced about his stay in Penang hill in the mid-19th century as follows: "We retire to a shady seat, commanding a panoramic view of the Kedah and Perak mountains and plains, the little islands, the narrow straits, the blue unbounded ocean. We turn again, and our eyes rest on the white glittering houses of the town, three thousand feet beneath the bands of intersecting roads, the clean regular nutmeg plantations, the scattered villages, and the green palm groves. Well has Penang earned the title of "Gem

Penang Hill's Tea Kiosk with its pergola porch

of the ocean", well has she incited her numerous poets to sing of her in rapturous lays".

Penang's hill station consists of many charming bungalows built in the 1920s, after the funicular service was introduced. The homes at the top of the hill belonged to planters and administrators, while those slightly lower down were mainly owned by Chinese towkays. The most prominent landmark is **The Great Wall** visible from the funicular train. At the very top is **Bel Retiro**, the governor's Hill Residence, the foundation of which dates from the early 1800s. The flagstaff here was used to signal to the flagstaff station at Fort Cornwallis, hence the official name of Penang Hill as Flagstaff Hill, i.e. Bukit Bendera. Another important 19th-century complex, in very original condition, is the **Christian Brothers' Bungalow** which was used as a retreat for the La Sallean Brothers and the schoolboys of Saint Xaviers' Institution.

In the early 1990s, the Friends of Penang Hill, led by the Consumers Association of Penang (CAP), mounted what is probably the region's largest environmental campaign to date, to save the Penang Hills from a proposed RM460 million development over 900 acres. The mega-development plans have been shelved, but the state still has plans for some hotel development and a cable car.

"The Friends" think that Penang Hill would be served better if it was conserved as a state nature park. They are also lobbying for improved access to the Hill by upgrading the railway. They have published an alternative plan in "Penang Hill; The Need to Save Our Natural Heritage". Amongst other information provided in the plan, the book lists the many endemic or rare species of plants on Penang Hill such as witch hazel (*Maingaya malayana*), the slipper orchid (*Paphiopedilum barbatum*), which has become rare because of over-collection and habitat destruction, and the monkey cup (*Nepthentes albomarginata*).

Penang Hill is also rich in bird life, with no less than 78 species of birds, some of which are rare species such as, the chestnut-capped thrush, the white-bellied woodpecker, the great-bearded bee eater and the red-throated sunbird. Small mammals like the tree shrew, civet cat, flying lemur, mouse deer, the long-tailed macaque, the dusky leaf monkey and the black giant squirrel are also found here.

There are two especially popular ways to walk up Penang Hill: the first, is a footpath starting from the **Moon Gate**, which is along Jalan Waterfall and a few hundred metres from the Botanic Gardens' entrance; and the second, a jeep road starting near the entrance to the Botanic Gardens. Both meet at **Eighty-four**, a shed serving fresh tea, coffee and biscuits, run by a volunteer group of veteran hill-climbers. The hike to the top of Penang Hill can take anything from just over an hour, for athletes, to three hours, for more ordinary mortals.

The hills are covered with an elaborate network of tracks, and one can hike from Ayer Itam to Balik Pualu or Teluk Bahang. These treks usually start out as footpaths, but worry not, civilization approaches; they soon become cemented trails for the farmers to transport their produce, and are finally transformed into motorcar roads leading to homes in the hills around Balik Pulau and Air Itam on the south and eastern sides of the hill range.

Round The Island
South to Bayan Baru, the Bayan Lepas Airport and round to Balik Pulau

From the Snake Temple in the midst of Malaysia's silicon valley, to a cultural experience at Kampung Seronok and Malay fishing villages. Balik Pulau, meaning "behind the island", is the rural side of Penang island. It is a small market town within a charming landscape of Malay architecture, fruit orchards, clove and nutmeg plantations.

Driving south along Jalan C.Y. Choy (Bridge Street) from George Town, and along Jalan Jelutong on the east coast of the island,you will pass through Jelutong and Gelugor, two areas that are named after trees. Jelutong was the earliest industrial area of George Town, dating from the turn of the century. Industries such as food-processing and ice-factories needed a large water supply and were situated next to the Pinang River.

The **Pinang River** was once an important waterway used by Achehnese, Malay and Tamil traders to sail up to the villages of the interior. Masjid Makbul, a mosque on the banks of the river, started out as a prayer hall and resting place for these traders. Its main tributaries are the Waterfall River (*Sungai Ayer Terjun*) and the Ayer Itam River.

Going south along Jalan Jelutong, on your right, at the Lorong Perak junction light, you will see a pleasant looking single-storey bungalow. Once the **house of Syed Shaikh al-Hadi**, the foremost Islamic modernist reformer of early 20th century Penang, this house is now occupied by vegetarian nuns who use it as a temple.

On Jalan Tunku Kudin, the coastal road which takes you to the Penang Bridge, look up and you may spot the ruins of **Rumah Tunku Kudin** or "**Udini House**" perched on top of a hill. Tunku Kudin was the controversial prince of Kedah who became entangled in the Selangor civil war in the 1860s and 1870s, during which he was backed by the British, and lost. With no political future in Kedah, Tunku

The ruins of Rumah Tengku Kudin (Jalan Tengku Kudin)

Kudin decided to retire permanently in Penang after 1882. He lived in this grand country home on the hill, keeping an aviary and free-roaming deer until his death in 1906. The mansion was later bought by Tunku Kudin's near namesake, Ku Din bin Ku Meh, the High commissioner of Setul in South Thailand. During the Japanese Occupations, the mansion was used as a Japanese naval base; more recently it has been occupied by the marine Police.

The **Penang Organic Farm Centre** (POF) is at Bukit Gelugor, just off Jalan Sultan Azlan Shah (Gelugor Road). The POF Centre is a sales outlet for organic fruits and vegetables, fresh bread and other eco-friendly products. Every Saturday night, a vegetarian dinner open to the public, is served. Established in 1992, the POF is the most successful organic enterprise in the country, with another farm near Sungai Pinang on the other side of the island.

The **University Science of Malaysia** (USM) campus was formerly a British military camp, commanding a good site on Bukit Minden. The university library is one of the best in the country, and

should be interesting to researchers who are here for a longer stay.

The **University Museum & Art Gallery** displays textiles, prints, traditional jewellery and keris. It also has an ethnographic and traditional performing arts section. Thanks to a generous endowment, the art gallery has managed to assemble a fine sampling of Malaysian modern art. Further south lie the trade fair grounds where the Pesta Pulau Pinang (Penang Festival) is held at the end of each year.

Bayan Baru, established in the early 1970s, is the **Penang De-**velopment Corporation's (PDC) first industrial township. Today it is a modern town centre with an extensive road system. The two main shopping malls, **Sunshine Square** and **Kompleks Bukit Jambul**, are surrounded by shoplots. The former became quickly successful as it was the first shopping complex built in the district. The latter, to serve the sourthern end of Bayan Baru, has a skating rink and a variety of retail and fast food outlets. Just outside are a host of restaurants and eating places serving all manner of foods.

The **PDC** office building is located in Bayan Baru. PDC's industrial division are the people to see to make inquiries on pioneer (tax-free) status benefits, factory space leases, the state's financial services available, as well as the manufacturing support and service capabilities of the region that is already in place in Penang. The PDC also has a tourism division and a housing division.

Just opposite PDC's office building is the **Penang International Sports Arena** (PISA), Penang's newest and largest sports stadium and convention venue.

The modernistic building of the Penang Development Corporation on Persiaran Mahsuri in Bayan Baru

The Penang International Sports Arena along Jalan Tun Dr. Awang in Bayan Baru

Built for the 1998 Commonwealth Games that was held in the country, the present management has made the sports complex into a centre of activity for the Bayan Baru community. Its competition and leisure pools are superbly maintained and are becoming a favoured place for families and locals to enjoy a swim and a meal. Its Main Arena and function rooms are popularly used for exhibitions, fairs, concerts, conventions, sporting events, banquets and corporate events. The use of its facilities which combine badminton, volleyball, sepak takraw, basketball courts and table tennis areas are also picking up. And its massive covered car park and grounds are now also being innovatively used for retail outlets and market fairs.

The development of a golf course and the **Hotel Equatorial Penang** (see page 95) next to it, in the hilly land of Bukit Jambul

Penang's "Bukit Jambul Orchid, Hibiscus & Reptile Garden"
Persiaran Bukit Jambul, 11900 Penang Malaysia
Tel (60-4) 644 8863   Fax (60-4) 644 2236

For enquiring minds, a large and fascinating variety of flora and reptilian fauna, including turtles, terrapins and iguana.

which adjoins Bayan Baru, were both initiated by the PDC to attract Japanese investors by offering opportunities for combining business with pleasure. Also in PDC's Bukit Jambul development, in the grounds of the International College, is the state government's new think tank for sustainable development, called the **Socio-Economic & Environmental Research Institute** (SERI Penang).

The Bukit Jambul Orchid, Hibiscus and Reptile Garden (see this page), also in Bukit Jambul, cultivates many varieties of hibiscus, Penang's state flower. The giant orchid, the *Grammatophyllum speciosum*, is a star attraction. Also on show are large turtles, terrapins, iguanas and the like. You may relish the thought of being photographed with a large Albino Python or the world's largest show tortoise.

Bayan Lepas Free Industrial Zone

The Bayan Lepas Free Industrial Park used to be padi fields as far as the eye could see. It is situated around the Kluang River (now canalised), which, in all early historical accounts, was, in addition

to Air Itam, the most fertile valley in Penang island. James Scott, Francis Light's trading partner, thought that Sungai Kluang would be a better site for a township than George Town, and that the harbour between Sungai Kluang and Pulau Jerejak would be a more suitable one for ship-building. He bought up much of the land in this area, speculating that the British trading post would be re-sited to "Jamestown", but lost his money on it. With no reference to that episode, almost two centuries later, Bandar Bayan Baru was founded on approximately the same site.

The process of industrialisation began almost thirty years ago when factories like Intel, Hewlett-Packard and Clarion were granted pioneer status (which allows for a number of tax-free years of operation) to set up manufacturing and assembly plants in Penang. The state government, through the PDC, acquired the padi fields, resettled the villagers, and converted agricultural land into a Free Industrial Zone (originally called the Free Trade Zone) for export manufacturing. Today, the PDC industrial parks have gained a reputation as the Silicon Valley of the East, with electronics-industry multinationals, such as Dell, Packard-Bell, Hewlett-Packard, Intel and Alcatel, establishing a strong presence here.

It is also at the Bayan Lepas FIZ that you can see how world-class fine jewellery is made at the OE factory. Here, Malaysian craftsmen handcraft jewellery in platinum and gold set with diamonds and other precious gems, to be exported to over 38 countries worldwide.

You will be fascinated with the complimentary guided factory

OE factory at Bayan Lepas

Rudolf Erdel Platinum

tour, which will take you through the various processes involved in jewellery- making. You will see skilled craftsmen working on intricate designs and the materials used. At the end of the tour, you will be taken to a showroom, where you will see over 1,500 innovative designs on display.

Among the pioneer factories in the area, OE was established in 1974 by its chairman, Mr Erich Oeding-Erdel, whose family has been in the jewellery business in Muenster, Germany since 1906. OE specializes in designing and manufacturing platinum and gold jewellery set with diamonds and other precious gems for the most demanding markets.

Its jewellery is available in leading jewellery stores in the USA,

Europe and Middle East, among others. Among its international brands are C-Natasha, Rudolf Erdel Platinum and Lillian Too's Feng Shui Fine Jewellery.

The OE factory is just a 10-minute drive from the Penang International Airport, Penang Bridge or Snake Temple. Guided tours are available from Mondays to Fridays, 9am - 5pm. For free transport and enquiries, call (604) 641 5715. In addition, daily demonstrations are available at all OE Fine Jewellery showrooms.

The **Snake Temple at Sungai Kluang** was built around 1850 in memory of a Buddhist priest and healer, Chor Soo Kong, whose birthday is celebrated on the sixth day of the *Chinese New Year* (around February). In its original setting, within a forest which served as a natural sanctuary, the snake temple inspired a sense of awe and mystery. With development of the surrounding area,

C-Natasha

OE Fine Jewellery showrooms in Malaysia

FACTORY & SHOWROOM:
Bayan Lepas FIZ 3, Penang
Tel : 04 - 641 5707

PENANG:
Lot 29-30 (2nd Floor) Island Plaza
118 Jalan Tanjung Tokong
Tel : 04 - 899 9880

KUALA LUMPUR:
P3 Prestige Floor
Lot 10 Shopping Centre
50 Jalan Sultan Ismail
Tel : 03 - 241 1688

Block A Seri Utama
Kuala Lumpur Craft Complex
Section 63 Jalan Conlay
Tel : 03 - 2162 3323

MALACCA:
No1 Jalan PM2, Plaza Mahkota
Bandar Hilir
Tel : 06 - 292 1818

ONLINE SHOWROOM
www.oewebstore.com.my

Craftsman at work

Visitors observing the process of jewellery-making at the OE factory

62

The Snake Temple at Sungai Kluang

have a model kampung house on show with memorabilia and traditional farming implements. There is also a purpose-built cultural venue for various performances.

From Kampung Seronok, a meandering drive eastwards will bring you to two fishing villages at "the end of the world", along the southeastern leg of Penang's turtle-shaped island.

The Malay fishing village of **Teluk Tempoyak Kecil** features an open-air restaurant on the waterfront with a large grill in full view of the customers. It's a community affair and the atmosphere is all the merrier for it. **Batu Maung**, the predominantly Chinese fishing village, has a seafood restaurant in an attap house on high stilts. Incidentally, at Batu Maung, there is a small shrine which marks what is supposedly a giant footprint left behind by Admiral Cheng Ho, who led the famous 15th-century Ming voyages to Southeast Asia.

however, few snakes remain at the temple now.

The temple was already an established tourist attraction when the playwright Noel Coward and his friend, the Earl of Amherst, visited Penang around 1930. Their visit is related by George Bilankain in "Hail, Penang". Looking conspicuously fashionable in "blue berets, white trousers, and tennis shirts open at the neck", the celebrities entered the temple and were at first disappointed to see nothing more than a few Straits Chinese women praying. "Suddenly Coward and Amherst recognised that parts of the furniture "were snakes, dark green in colour, five-six-and-seven-feet-long, with triangular heads. They were coiled round candle sticks, hanging loosely from bells, entwined about sundry small gods, surrounding the earthenware pots in which joss sticks are places after prayer. Coward stroked the body of one snake while Amherst showed more normal respect for unknown reptiles... ."

You can take a road behind the Penang International Airport in Bayan Lepas to some interesting villages.

The first is **Kampung Seronok.** The name "Village of Enjoyment" was given by an English engineer who observed the villagers' merry-making shortly after the Japanese occupation and during the British re-occupation of Malaya. Kampung Seronok is a splendid example of how a traditional village has employed tourism to develop its own cultural and economic resources. Led by an authoritative headman or penghulu, the villagers are given daily routines, which include keeping the village clean. For their efforts, they have won a "cleanest village prize" from a sponsored competition.

The villagers have also developed an amazing variety of projects. The core industry is a printing press called Sinaran Brothers. In addition, they have managed to keep their paddy fields while most of the rice-growing land on the island has been converted for industrial use. They have taken up the rearing of fowl and rabbits and have integrated an aqua-farm for breeding gourmet fish. They have started a library, and the children take part in cultural dance groups and orchestras for gamelan, classical music and band music. They

On the round island road, after Jalan Sultan Azlan Shah and past the Penang airport in Bayan Lepas, you can go to **Teluk Kumbar**. The attraction here is a stall at the jetty near the police station which serves mee udang - prawn mee with very large prawns. From Teluk Kumbar, the south coast road will then take you to the fishing village of **Gertak Sanggul**.

This coastal drive takes you past Penang's rural landscape of traditional Malay villages and some good beaches. At Teluk Kumbar, you can elect to take the northbound road to the town of Balik Pulau. However, a much shorter way to get there from George Town is from Air Itam, via the new Jalan Relau which passes over

Balik Pulau town cente

on Organic Farms). The POF people also practice some form of LETS (Local Employment and Trading System) or barter trade. The vegetables are sold at the POF Centre in Gelugor.

Moving north from Sungai Pinang, you can get to Teluk Bahang, passing by an attractive waterfall area with deep pools for swimming, called Air Terjun Titi Kerawang. A number of roadside stalls mark this popular picnicking spot. From the stalls, you can see examples of durian, clove nutmeg, cocoa and pepper plants.

the central hills.

Balik Pulau

Balik Pulau is a market town with one main street, in the middle of which is a drinking fountain presented in 1882 by Koh Seang Tat, a Chinese plantation owner. The town is surrounded by clove, nutmeg, rubber and durian estates. An old Catholic church and convent form part of the heritage of the Hakka community here.

The original inhabitants of Balik Pualu were Malays from Kedah and Perlis to the north of Penang, as well as from Pattani, Setul and Yala in South Thailand. These people fled here in the 18th and 19th century because their provinces were attacked or threatened by Siamese forces. Not far from Balik Pulau is a charming Malay village called Sungai Rusa, with some excellent examples of Malay architecture.

The District and Land Office for the Southwest District was and still is located in Balik Pulau. The premises of the District and Land Office is a double-storey building from the 1880s. Before the Japanese Occupation, the District Office was a microcosm of British administration. The ground floor was occupied by the post and telegraph office as well as offices for customs and excise, the opium clerk, the agricultural department and the irrigation department. On the upper floor was a courthouse with Indian and Chinese court interpreters, and an administrative division.

Sungai Pinang

The town of Sungai Pinang (not to be confused with the Sungai Pinang or Pinang River in George Town) has a temple, a school, a market and a main street with shophouses. From here it is not far to the Penang Organic Farm (POF), but be prepared for a 45-minute climb. Call (604) 657 5591 beforehand to ask for directions.

The POF has a four-acre site located 1,000 feet above sea level, enjoying a panoramic view of Penang's west coast. The farm is run entirely by volunteers. Eco-tourists may drop in for a day or stay on for several weeks, receiving free food and lodging in return for their labour. Some learn about it through an international network called WWOOF (Willing Workers

Pantai Acheh Forest Reserve

From Sungai Pinang, the west or leftward turn is the road to Pantai Acheh. This north-western part of Penang island is the Pantai Acheh Forest Reserve. Apart from the hill water catchment areas, the Pantai Acheh Forest Reserve is the only relatively undisturbed lowland forest left on the island.

Pantai Acheh Forest Reseve has a diverse eco-system, from sandy beach to rocky coast, lowland to hill dipterocarp forests. The beach of Pantai Kerachut here boasts a lake where sea water meets fresh stream water. The sandy beach is the nesting site for two of the seven remaining species of sea turtles in the world. The Green Turtles (Chelonia mydas) nest between the months of April to August, followed by the Olive-Ridley (Lepidochelys olivacea) from September to February.

With the significant eco-tourism potential of the forest reserve, the Malaysian Nature Society is now campaigning for the Pantai Acheh Forest Reserve to be gazetted into a State Park to protect it from any form of development.

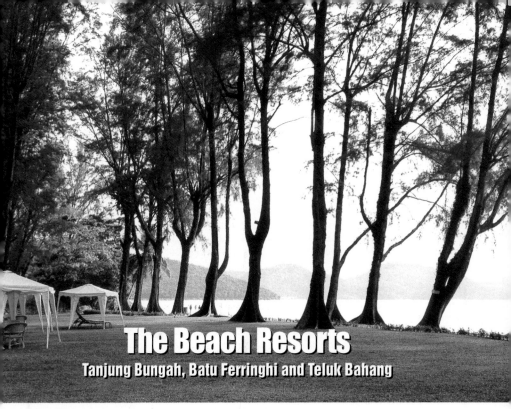

The Beach Resorts
Tanjung Bungah, Batu Ferringhi and Teluk Bahang

Since the early 1970s when the first five-star hotel in Southeast Asia was established on the Batu Feringghi stretch of beach, Penang has earned its popularity as a modern international tourist resort. It offers tourists not only sun and sea but also an appealing mix of other elements - good hotel facilities, great food, friendly people, casual shopping and a relaxed atmosphere.

As a general rule, the further west you go along the north beach, the better the beaches are. The best are now monopolised by international hotels, but in fact all beaches are open to the public, even if access may be limited.

Tanjung Tokong

One of the first of the beach suburbs along the northern coastline is Tanjung Tokong, which means "Temple Cape". It was, originally, a small Chinese fishing village, with a Malay *kampung* (village), a little to the south-west of it.

The **Tua Pek Kong Temple**, after which the cape was named, still guards the fishing village now hidden behind some low-cost Urban Development Authority flats on your way west to the Chinese Swimming Club on the north beach road. Each year, on the eve of the fifteenth day of *Chinese New Year* (around February), a flame-watching ritual takes place here.

The village was a favourite picnic spot before World War II and is still a popular place to eat charcoal-baked crabs today.

The Malay *kampung* crowns the large Fettes Park residential suburb which was developed to house Royal Australian Air Force personnel in the early 60s. A land reclamation project based on tide flows is underway from Tanjung Tokong to Gurney Drive, so the beach front across the road from the kampung is a creeping land fill. The hill side of Tanjung Tokong is **Mount Erskine** which is site to a large Chinese burial ground, established in the early 1800s. The best preserved cemetery here is the **Cheah cemetery**, one of the first on your left if you drive along Jalan Mount Erskine from Jalan Burma in Pulau Tikus. Some of the burial land has been redeveloped for highrise apartments, among them a private burial ground where the **Khoo Soo Hong mausoleum** from around 1895 is found.

Like many of the "villages" on the island, Tanjung Tokong is a growing township.

Along the north coast road, around the traffic light intersection where the beach road meets the road to the Fettes Park housing estate, a major commercial area is being very much improved.

The core of the new commercial area is the Island Plaza shopping complex which initiated the renewal of the area now underway.

Adjacent to and just across the IPSC's access road, there is the **Disc & Dat** original music CD and Laserdisc centre, as well as more eating places and retail outlets. With its extensive range of original music CDs, the Disc & Dat (see page 111) attracts most of Penang's music enthusiasts for their CD collections and gift purchases.

Directly opposite the IPSC, along the main coast road, a just completed shophouse mall complex promises to enhance still further the growth of this north coast suburb.

Tanjung Bungah

As you move west into Tanjung Bungah ("Flower Cape") from the Tanjung Tokong traffic light junction, you will pass the **Penang Chinese Swimming Club**, haw-ker eateries, flourishing new hotels, condominiums and service apartments.

Saint John's Hill, at Jalan Cengai (off Jalan Gajah, just opposite the Penanag Chinese Swimming Club), is where **Mariophile**, an early 19th century Anglo-Indian building belonging to the Catholic Church's **College General**, is to be found.

The College General was a regional seminary which relocated

The bustling development at the junction to the Fettes Park residential estate in Tanjung Tokong promises more activity in this once sleepy fishing village.

The beginning of the coast road to Tanjung Bungah and Batu Ferringhi is undergoing great change as shown as shown by this approach to the Fettes Park residential estate at Tanjung Tokong

to Penang in 1808, and Mariophile is its old retreat. The former was a large complex at Gurney Drive, demolished about ten years ago amidst some protests.

According to the writer Milton Osborne a Vietnamese scholar named Petrus Truong Vinh Ky studied at the College General from 1852-58. He later became something like the father of modern Vietnamese press during the French colonial period. Weld wrote in 1880 that he visited this "French College for Foreign Missions" in Penang, where he found "a large number of pupils of many nationalities - Latin being the tongue in common use."

Going further west along the beach road, you come to **Paradise Tanjung Bungah** (see page 103), which is the first of the stretch of Tanjung Bungah beach hotels. From here, the beach road

passes the **Penang Swimming Club** before it takes you to Hillside and the remainder of the Tanjung Bungah beach hotels.

Development of the large housing estate called Hillside, recognisable from the 7-Eleven outlet on the left from the beach road, was largely fueled by the housing needs of the Royal Australian Air Force (RAAF) servicemen and their families in the 1960s and 70s, as they relocated from less comfortable quarters. Today, it is one of the better residential suburbs for all communitites. The Hillside entry way from the main beach road also winds up a little hillock, called Pearl Hill, which has become a favoured place for detached residences.

On the sea side opposite Hillside are the remaining Tanjung Bungah beach hotels, all of which were developed to provide a resort al-

ternative closer to the city. The first of these is the **Copthorne Orchid Penang** (see page 102), followed by the **Paradise Sandy Bay** (see page 103), and the **Crown Prince Hotel.**

The Copthorne's **SHOCK Egypt Discotheque** appears to have taken radical steps to break away from the trend towards techno-music and its drug-related connotations. Instead, this popular discotheque, open six days a week from 9pm to 3am, is actively promoting healthy fun by spinning mostly R&B music. Providing Penangites and visitors with yet another option for their evenings out.

Separating the Copthorne and Paradise Sandy Bay beach hotels is **Dalat School,** an American missionary school that was relocated years ago from Dalat, Vietnam. And continuing on past the

67

Shangri-La's Rasa Sayang Resort

beach hotels, you come to Tanjung Bungah town proper.

This small town is a simple T-junction with the Tanjong Bungah bus-stop as its main point of importance. The goreng pisang (fried banana) stall here is famous among locals. On the sea side is the original fishing village at **Pantai Remis**, located in fact, along a deep bay. Several old seaside restaurants, like Hollywood, which offer open air dining under the sea almond trees, are still popular.

From the town, the narrow winding road to Batu Ferringhi offers glimpses of sandy beaches on one side while forested hills climb up almost immediately to the left of it. Work is in progress to widen the road due to the recent steep increase in traffic, but given the needs of current usage, this process is necessarily slow.

Batu Ferringhi

Batu Ferringhi, the "Portuguese Rock" which protrudes dramatically at the point of an estuary, was where Portuguese ships stopped for fresh water. The Portuguese never colonised Penang, but this romantic stretch of Batu Ferringhi beach has nevertheless become a favoured holiday site today. The Batu Ferringhi beaches are among the best in Penang and

Rasa Sayang's pool and slide

this is where the resort hotels are concentrated.

On both sides of the beach road along Batu Ferringhi, a large number of restaurants and shops have opened next to the hotels. Most of these are purpose-built to cater for the package tourist and are easily recognised by their size and bright lights. Then, there is the **Yahong Gallery** (see page 111), established by the family of the doyen of batik painters, Chuah Thean Teng, which sells paintings, and a broad range of artifacts, souvenirs and curios. At the end of the lane next to the **Penang Parkroyal Resort** is the Bayu Senja complex, an open-air gallery of stalls for small entrepreneurs, where you can find hand-painted T-shirts and good pizza.

Many of the hotels organise short hikes up the hill for tourists to get a feel for the tropical rainforest.

The Rasa Sayang's superb beach front

One of these hikes goes up to **Chin Farm Waterfall**, a gentle cascade which is popular with the locals.

For those who prefer a gentle uphill stroll, the best trek is along the **Batu Ferringhi Aquaduct**. It is relatively undisturbed and a favourite among birdwatchers. Permission from the Penang Water Authority can usually be organised by your hotel if you are staying at one of the beach hotels.

The *grande dame* of Batu Feringghi is **Shangri-La's Rasa Sayang Resort** (see pages 99 and 100), which 25 years ago catapulted Penang to fame with the island's first beach resort in the region with five-star status. The Rasa Sayang (which connotes "the love of life and all its pleasures") has aged well, and enjoys one of the highest rates of repeat guests in the Malaysian hotel industry.

The resort's architecture incorporates a distinctive Minangkabau roof. The building design blends well with the environment, having adhered to an old guideline which requires Batu Feringghi buildings to be no taller than the surrounding trees.

The resort was recently refurbished and expanded. The extensive new garden wing was designed around the spreading old rain trees which date from far before the resort was built. A delightful wooden tree house, incorporated into a particularly large rain tree, is a favourite attraction for both children and adults. From the tree house, a water slide descends into a multi-form swimming pool.

The luscious landscaped gardens at the Rasa Sayang Resort are lovingly cared for by the head gardener, who is also the hotel's longest serving employee. He started

service over twenty years ago as a bricklayer during the construction of the original resort.

The people who used to occupy the land on which the resort is now situated were relocated to another spot further up the Batu Feringghi main road. Their village has been adopted by the Rasa Sayang Resort, and the settlement has now been renamed **Kampung Rasa Sayang**. A "traditional kampung experience" is occasionally organised for the hotel's guests to allow them to meet the local villagers.

The Shangri-La's Rasa Sayang Resort operates a shuttle service linking its sister hotels, **Golden Sands Resort** and the **Shangri-La Hotel** in the heart of George Town. Hotel guests can enjoy the facilities of all three hotels, inclusive of cross-signing privileges. The beach in front of Rasa Sayang Resort and the neighbouring Golden Sands Resort boasts

69

Roadside stalls in Batu Ferringhi

a fine bed of sand. This popular stretch of beach offers batik-printing demonstrations, horse rides for children, and a wide range of water sports such as jet-ski boating, speed boating, banana boating, hang gliding and parasailing. You can also book a one-hour motor boat ride to Coral Island for snorkeling, or a shorter ride to the nearby Pantai Kerachut.

The usual beach tourist activities combine a round-the-island-tour, souvenir shopping, trekking up the forested hillside, cycling and sunbathing on the beach. All three of the Shangri-La's group of hotels have good communication, gym and swimming pool facilities. You'll also find a wide varitey of food and beverage outlets.

Within the vicinity of the Rasa Sayang, there are a large number of restaurants and shops, in addition to numerous night-market stalls selling a wide range of souvenirs. In the evening, it is pleasant to browse among these little stalls along the road although the side-walks are somewhat narrow. Prices are reasonable if you know how to bargain. Imitation watches, small art-works, costume jewel-

lery, batik clothes, beachwear, crafts and memorabilia are all uninhibitedly displayed and peddled. Some have questioned the legality of these shops, but with bargains this good, it is best not to ask too many questions. *

Continuing west from the Rasa Sayang, you have the Shangri-La's **Golden Sands Resort** (see pages 99), followed by the **Holiday Inn, Parkroyal, Lone Pine**, and **Bayview** beach hotels, before you come to the vintage **Casuarina Beach Resort Penang** (see page 102). Both, the Golden Sands and Casuarina are well-liked for their more intimate sizes, with family groups favouring the Sands for its varied activities, and the more adult crowd, the Casuarina for its quiet ambience.

Teluk Bahang

Teluk Bahang, the "Bay of Glowing Embers" at the westernmost tip of Penang island, is blessed with a beautiful sunset and a superb stretch of beach. There is still a major fishing village, with a fisherman's pier going out a distance into the sea. The Malay kampung still maintains a traditional social

ambience, with children, chickens and cats scurrying underneath the raised timber houses.

Located on Teluk Bahang's prime beachfront is the **Penang Mutiara Beach Resort** (see page 97), the only member of the Leading Hotels of the World in Penang.

Designed to be the ultimate beach resort, no expense was spared to create the ultimate in luxury tropical beach accommodation for the Mutiara. The landscaped grounds are generously filled with an extensive variety of tropical blooms and flora. And the building design, with large expanses of glass, makes the resort's interior one with its green exterior.

This pride in the beauty of the resort's views are fully exploited in the Penang Mutiara's design.

All guestrooms boast balconies that overlook its grounds and command breathtaking ocean views at the same time. Bougainvillaea blooms tumble around your breakfast and tea table, and one of the world's most stunning sunsets form a backdrop to early-evening cocktails.

Comfort and service was made a resort priority when modern luxury was mixed with age old Asian traditions of service. Ware wooden shutters and exotic fabrics lend an air of timeless elegance to its guestrooms.

The bathrooms are unique, say many of their guests. Each comes with twin basins, separate shower cubicles and a deep tub, with abundant marble, chrome and glass creating a refreshing and cool retreat.

Planned as a true escape from the world, your way to the landscaped

The Penang Mutiara beachfront is arguably one of the best in Penang

Lounge", where glass walls on three sides of the lounge offer a panoramic view of the garden, sea and the blue horizon, is a great place to sip tea or cocktails. Alternatively, you can also relax over a pre-dinner drink with friends at the "**Puppetry Lounge**", located adjacent to La Farfalla, and enhanced with *wayang kulit* puppets depicted on etched mirrors.

Although the Penang Mutiara prides itself on being a beach resort par excellence, its comprehensive range of meeting rooms and state-of-the-art convention facilities also make it an ideal venue for business meetings and conferences. Outdoor dining and stylish theme parties are a house speciality.

swimming pool takes you past ponds which are home to flamingos, mandarin ducks and coloured koi carp. This setting is complemented by a cool, poolside sculpture of dolphins.

Located as it is at the end of Penang's northern beach coastline, the resort needs to be quite self contained. The Penang Mutiara, consequently, is home to a large number of specialised food outlets.

Its **Garden Terrace** outlet is an ideal choice for breakfast, a leisurely lunch or a starlit dinner overlooking the pool. It provides a comprehensive selection of Asian and international fare at any hour.

Then, there is "**The House of Four Seasons**" where Chinese culinary specialities - Cantonese and Szechuan are served in an elegant setting recalling all the opulence of Old China.

At the resort's "**La Farfalla**", European dining room, the finest Italian dishes are presented amidst elegant works of art, etched in

glass which divide the room into intimate, private dining areas. La Farfalla has captured several awards including the Best Western Food Restaurant by Tourism Malaysia, Best Restaurant in Penang's Tourism Awards and the Top 10 Malaysian Restaurants by Flavours Magazines.

Then there is the "**Tsuru-Noya**", which serves authentic Japanese cuisine and is reached by a stroll through a landscaped garden.

On the other hand, the "**Palmetto**

With its superb beachfront, you can enjoy a swim in the sea, go para-sailing, laze on the beach, or borrow a bicycle to explore the jungle trails across the beach road.

For those who wish to explore, Teluk Bahang has quite a few places they can visit. Within a 2 minute walk from the hotel is the **Pinang Cultural Centre** which provides a comprehensive display

Penang Mutiara's Garden Terrace

The Batik factory allows visitors to view how *batik* is made

Muka Head

Muka Head is the northwestern leg, beyond Teluk Bahang, of the Penang island turtle. The coastline here is an expansive stretch of glittering sand interspersed with secluded coves within the shelter of gigantic rocks.

There are two, still quite pristine, beaches here - **Monkey beach** and **Pantai Kerachut**. They are accessible by boats which can be hired from the Penang Mutiara's watersports operator or via a hike from Teluk Bahang. The nearby islands are great for snorkelling and swimming.

The Muka Head lighthouse is located atop a cliff 785 feet high. The equipment for lighthouse was originally installed around the turn of the century by the Chance Brothers of Smethwick, Birmingham. In 1954, the same firm converted the petroleum vapour mantle-burners to high-power electric lamps. The installation of equipment was made the arduous way - "five trips a day by Chinese labourers".

of Malaysian tradition and culture. The Pinang Culture Centre operates 3 cultural tours daily (except Fridays) from 9.30 am to 5.00 pm.

From the Mutiara, a two hundred metre drive west on the beach road will also bring you to one of the oldest roundabouts in the region. And, taking a left there will take you to a **batik factory**, just half a kilometre away. *Batik* is cloth dyed by a wax-resistant method. The wax is painted on by hand or stencilled. The factory's shop offers a variety of *batik* material as well as ready made clothes. There is also a showroom parading a wide variety of *batik* paintings and other souvenirs. Besides this, guests can see how *batik* is made. *

The **Penang Butterfly Farm**, just a kilometre up the road from the batik factory, is a 20-minute walk from the Mutiara Beach Resort.

Opened in 1986, it is the first tropical butterfly farm in the world, and, covering an area of 0.8 hectares, is arguably the largest in the world. The Farm is home to 3000 living specimens of colourful butterflies, frogs, scorpions and other insects.

Most of the round-the-island tours stop at the batik factory and butterfly farm.

Another place to visit around Teluk Bahang is the **Forestry Museum**. Located a few kilometres south of the butterfly farm, the small museum is constructed with various species of wood and other forest produce, and is part of the 100-hectare **Teluk Bahang Forest Recreation Park**. It also houses a forest collection from all over the Malaysia.

The park itself features foot paths and a flowing stream, with a picnicking area by the stream that is popular among the locals.

Past this point, the road goes to the just completed Teluk Bahang dam, built in a forested valley. And after this is a tropical fruit farm of over 25 acres which offers 140 types of tropical and sub tropical fruits. The view from the farm is grand and you may get the chance to watch an Orang Asli Show as well.

Should you continue along this road, you will reach Balik Pulau. Otherwise, refer to pages 74-76, which guides your approach to the

Seberang Prai
Malay villages and plantations on mainland Penang

Across the Penang Bridge, on mainland Penang, are the sprawling housing estates, bright new shopping malls and booming industrial parks spread out along the modernising corridor of the North-South Highway. In contrast to these, the vast landscape of Malay villages, padi fields and old market centres of former plantation towns recall a less hurried age.

Penang state consists of Penang island and Seberang Prai on the mainland. These two parts of Penang state are linked together by a ferry service and the 13.5 kilometre **Penang Bridge**. The RM800 million bridge, completed in 1985, is still one of the longest in Asia. The ride from the island to the mainland is free, but the car toll for the journey back across the bridge is RM7.00.

Across the channel from George Town, where the ferry terminal meets the railway station, lies the new old town of Butterworth. The railway takes you north to Padang Besar and Bangkok, and south to Ipoh, Kuala Lumpur and Singapore. The small port has been superseded by the North Butterworth Container Terminal which handles most of Penang's bulk shipping trade today. The **Royal Australian Air Force** (RAAF) base in Butterworth is distinguished by an old fighter jet mounted as a sculpture in its front compound.

Seberang Prai, or **Province Wellesly**, is more similar to the other northern states of peninsular Malaysia, with a rural landscape punctuated by Malay villages. Some of the best scenery - traditional houses at the foot of tall coconut trees surrounded by green rice fields - can be seen north of Butterworth, at Penaga and along the trunk road to Kedah.

When Siam invaded Kedah in 1821, many of the Kedah Malays including the Sultan himself fled across the border and sought refuge in the British colony. A significant number settled permanently in Se-

Mengkuang Dam, site of the 1999 International Dragon Boat Race

St. Anne's Church in the outskirts of Bukit Mertajam

berang Prai. While the population of Seberang Prai is predominantly Malay, the towns are nevertheless Chinese-dominated, as is the case throughout much of Malaysia. In the 19th century, some areas were cleared for plantations - first sugar-cane, then coconut, and finally rubber. The historic plantation communities are predominantly Teochew Chinese or Christian Hakkas.

In more recent times, the Malay villages have been cleared for industrial estates, new townships and even golf courses. The main industrial township is **Seberang Jaya**, sited at the intersection of the North-south Highway and the East-West Highway. Seberang Jaya now boasts one of the state's largest mosque, the new state library, the Penang Bird Park and a large shopping complex.

The five-acre **Penang Bird Park** holds a collection of over 800 birds from more than 300 species. It features walk-in aviaries, landscaped ponds with water birds, Japanese carp and lilies. Although ornithologists may prefer to watch birds in more natural surroundings, the park is popular with

school children and family groups.

Several miles into the interior is **Bukit Mertajam**, a small old town at the railway intersection which connects Butterworth to the west, Padang Besar to the north, and Ipoh and Kuala Lumpur to the south. The road east to Kulim in Kedah also passes through. Bukit Mertajam is often called "smugglers' town", as it is a notorious source of liquor and other merchandise whose legality is somewhat debatable. The old town has several Chinese associations.

The **Saint Anne's Church** on the Jalan Kulim trunk road was built in 1957, replacing an older one which was built in 1888 but declared out of bounds during the Emergency period because it was suspected of being a communist hideout. The Emergency was a twelve-year period in Malaysia's history, over which a communist insurgency was successfully suppressed by the government. The nine-day *Saint Anne's feast* shuttling between the old church and the new, attracts a quarter million devotees. It climaxes in a candle-light procession by night on July 26.

The inscribed stone of **Cherok Tok Kun** stands in the grounds of Saint Anne's Church. The ancient Palli inscription, apparently dating from around the 4th century, reads "I acknowledge the enemies of the contented king Ramaunibba and the wicked are ever afflicted". Later on, Chinese, Jawi, Tamil and English inscriptions were also added. Lieutenant Colonel James Low, who investigated reports by local residents about this antiquity, recorded the inscriptions for posterity - some of which have weathered away - but could not resist adding his own mark "J. Low 1845".

Not far from Saint Anne's Church is the 37-acre **Bukit Mertajam Recreational Park**. Its jungle walks and picnic areas are popular with the locals.

To the north of Bukit Mertajam is the **Madrasah Manabi' Al-'Ulum** at Penanti. Shaikh 'Uthman Jalalludin was a religious scholar and author who studied in Mecca. Originating from Kelantan, he was also a pupil of the renowned Sufi teacher Tok Kenali. When in Mecca, he was invited by a devout couple to come back and set

Entrance to the Inner Court of the Kee Clan House in Sungai Bakap

up school in Penanti, Bukit Mertajam. Established by 1932, "The School Where Knowledge Shines" continues to attract students from all over Malaya, Indonesia and Thailand to the scenic countryside of Bukit Mertajam. The scholars' colony consists of a dense cluster of small thatched huts, whereas the school complex itself is sizeable, incorporating a three-storey building of fine timber craftsmanship.

The **Mengkuang Dam** near Bukit Mertajam is the largest in Penang, but most of its catchment area is situated across the border in Kedah. The dam is capable of storing more than 23,000 million litres and supplies most of Penang's water needs. Locals come for walks around the dam, and the annual dragon boat races are now held in the manmade lake.

At **Pagar Teras** you can see the ruins of the Sacred Heart, a large Catholic Church building erected in 1882. The Church was the centre of a Hakka plantation community until people were forced to relocate to Macang Bubuh during the Emergency.

The island of **Batu Kawan** is undergoing tremendous changes. It is soon to be converted into a light industrial park and housing estate with the largest sports stadium in Penang. Up till now it has been a palm oil plantation. The Brown Family first opened a sugar plantation but the crop failed when the island was inundated by a very high tide. J.M.B. Vermont and his brother John subsequently took over the management.

Just off the trunk road to the south is the **Kee Clan House at Sungai Bakap**, along the town's main street. The progenitor of the clan was Kee Lye Huat, a 19th-century sugar planter. The main building is an ancestral hall, behind which stand six large terrace houses built for the families of Kee Lye Huat's six sons. The two daughters and their husbands were given houses at either end of the main street. Several of the houses are still partially furnished, and some of the sugar farming implements have survived.

The Kee Clan House, placed under a family trust, is one of Penang's cultural treasures. In 1991, it was used as a set for the French film "Indo-Chine". Today, one of the many prominent Kees from this family is the State Minister for Tourism, Dato' Kee Phaik Cheen. Outspoken though Dato' Kee may be, regrettably, female Kees have no say in the running of the trust.

Sungei Petani in Kedah

With the completion of the peninsular's North-South Expressway, rapid change has come to the padi lands on either side of it. The previously sleepy township of Sungei Petani is a telling case in point.

The demand for residential space to house the explosive growth in people who can afford them in Kedah saw a radical transformation of Sungei Petani into the major Kedah township that it is today.

From a simple "cowboy" town, mostly straddling the old "trunk" road, Sungei Petani sprawls for kilometres all round the old town centre today. With new shopping complexes, cinemas, restaurants and bustling activity common to a large township.

Capping the new building going on is the Sungei Petani's **Strand Hospital & Retirement Home** (see page 107) which brings specialist medical care with a twist to the region, providing as it does, a building wing for retirees who may need a little care even as they enjoy their retired status.

With burgeoning industrial programmes, golf course and club developments taking place all around it, Sungei Petani's growth is not expected to slow down any time soon.

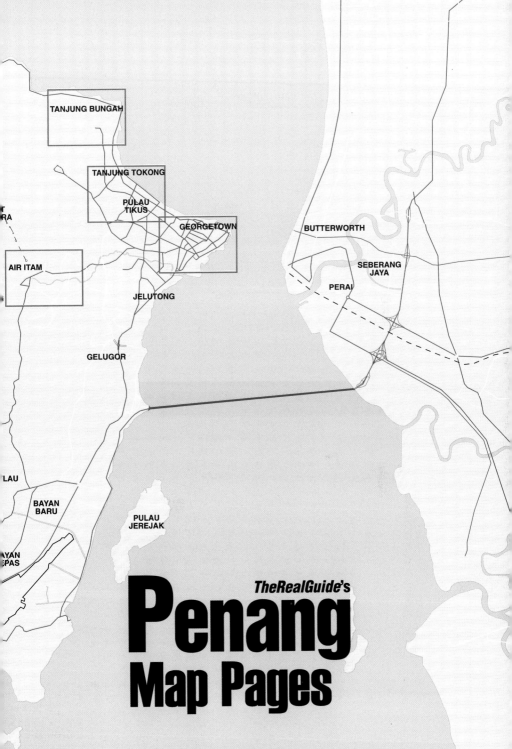

TANJUNG BUNGAH

TANJUNG TOKONG

PULAU TIKUS

GEORGETOWN

BUTTERWORTH

SEBERANG JAYA

PERAI

AIR ITAM

JELUTONG

GELUGOR

LAU

BAYAN BARU

PULAU JEREJAK

AYAN EPAS

TheRealGuide's

Penang
Map Pages

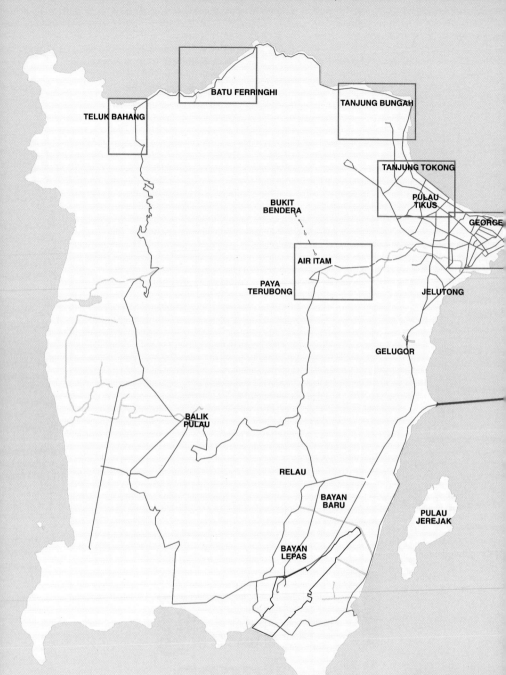

TELUK BAHANG

BATU FERRINGHI

TANJUNG BUNGAH

TANJUNG TOKONG

PULAU
TIKUS

GEORGE

BUKIT
BENDERA

AIR ITAM

PAYA
TERUBONG

JELUTONG

GELUGOR

BALIK
PULAU

RELAU

BAYAN
BARU

PULAU
JEREJAK

BAYAN
LEPAS

Penang Island

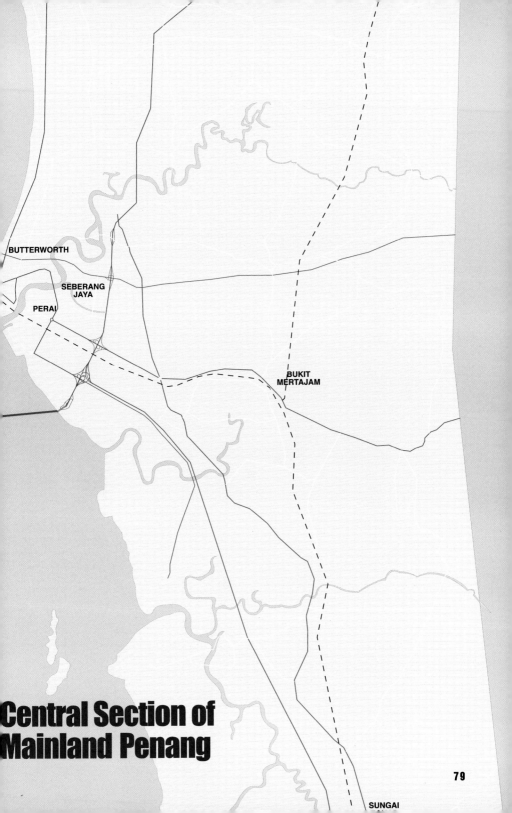

BUTTERWORTH

SEBERANG
JAYA

PERAI

BUKIT
MERTAJAM

Central Section of
Mainland Penang

SUNGAI

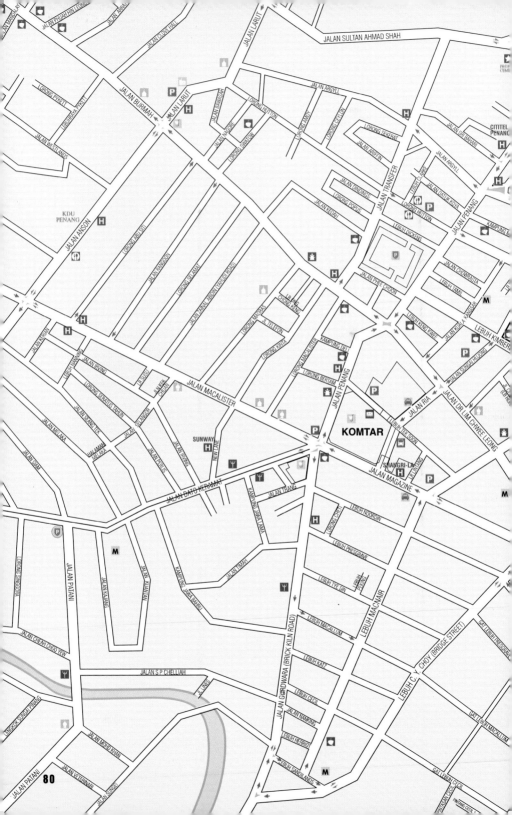

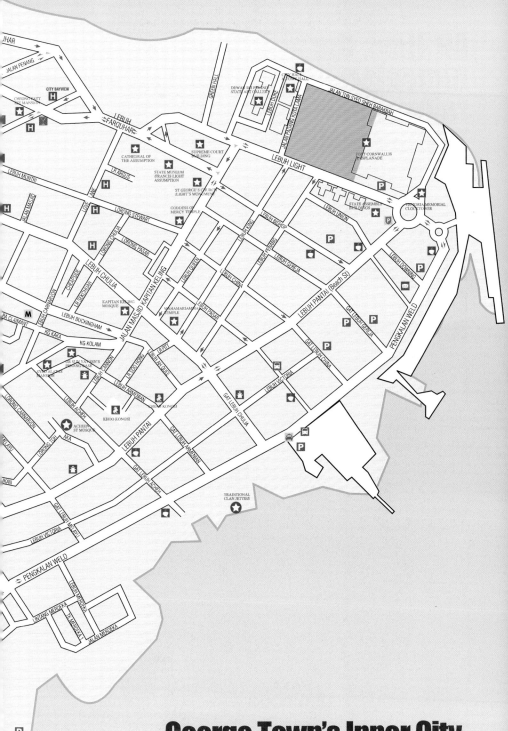

George Town's Inner City

Air Itam, the funicular railway Hill Station and the Paya Terubong road South to Bayan Lepas and Balik Pulau

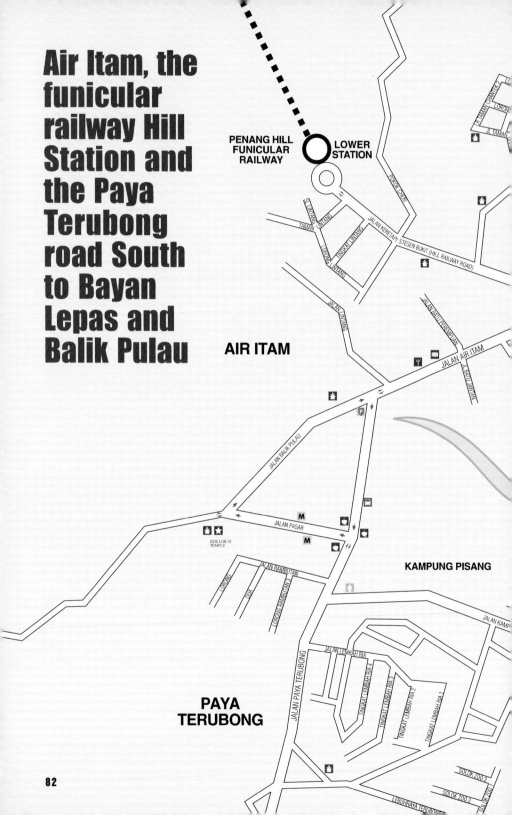

PENANG HILL FUNICULAR RAILWAY

LOWER STATION

JALAN KERETAPI STESEN BUKIT (HILL RAILWAY ROAD)

TAMAN LINTANG

TINGKAT LINTANG

LORONG LINTANG

JALAN LINTANG

JALAN BATU FERRINGHI

AIR ITAM

JALAN AIR ITAM

BATU PANTAI

JALAN BALIK PULAU

JALAN PASAR

M

M

KEK LOK SI TEMPLE

KAMPUNG PISANG

JALAN KAMP

JALAN RAMBUTAN

LORONG

DUA

LORONG RAMBUTAN 3

JALAN LEMBAH RIA

JALAN PAYA TERUBONG

TINGKAT LEMBAH RIA 4

TINGKAT LEMBAH RIA 3

TINGKAT LEMBAH RIA 2

TINGKAT LEMBAH RIA 1

PAYA TERUBONG

SOLOK ZOO 3

SOLOK ZOO 2

LEBUHRAYA TERUBONG

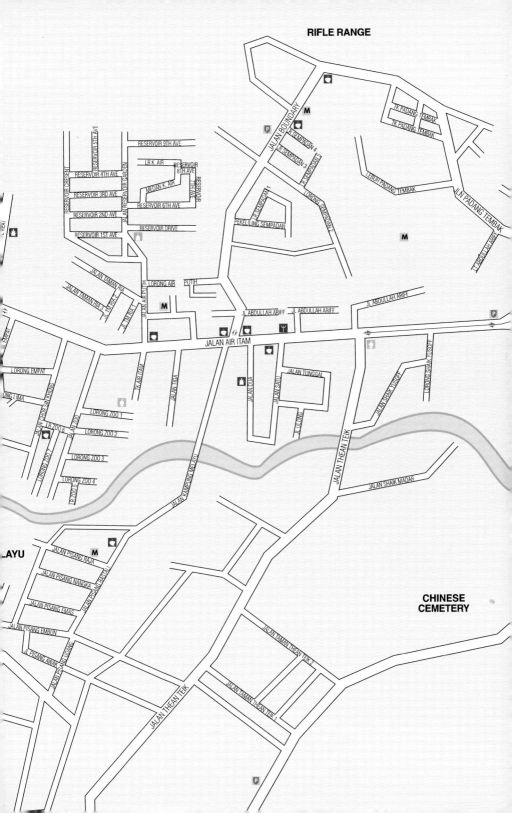

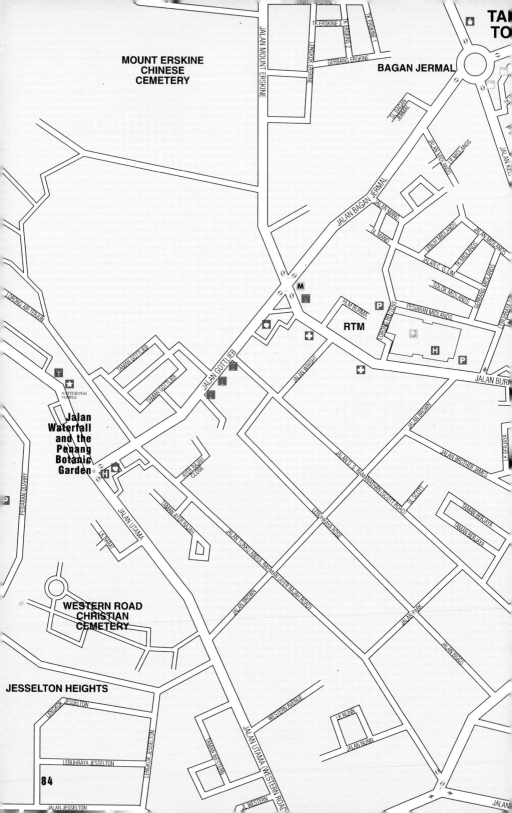

North coast roads and suburbs including Persiaran Gurney, Jalan Kelawei, Jalan Burmah up to Pulau Tikus, the start of Jalan Tanjung Tokong in the north and the Jalan Gottlieb, Jalan Utama junction to the Botanic Gardens in the east.

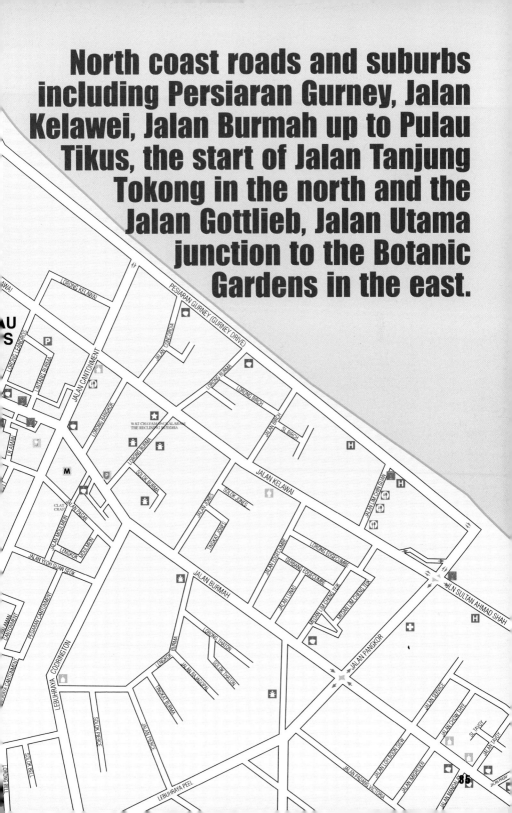

TANJUNG BUNGAH

LR ABRAS 2

JLN LR ABRAS

JALAN ABRAS

H PARADISE
TANJUNG BUNGAH

TANJUNG BUNGAH PARK

TANJUNG BUNGAH PARK

JALAN C M HASHIM

JL TOKONG
THAI PAK KONG

JALAN MERANTI

JL BUNGA
MATAHARI

JALAN MERBAU

JL BUNGA
PISANG

JALAN CHENGAI

JL BUNGA CHANDANGSARI

JL CHIONING

CHENG KEAN

LORONG BINTANG 2

JL BUNGA RAAPAT

JL BUNGA RAKYAWALI

JL BUNGA TANJUNGSARI

LR BT 3

JALAN GAJAH

JL BUNGA MAWAR

JALAN BINTANG

JALAN BUNGA TANJUNG

MUTIARA DUA

MEDAN FETTES

JALAN BINTANG

JL SAKORAI

JL LIM LIEW SAIK

JALAN ROSA

KACA PIRING

JALAN BUNGA TANJUNG

JALAN TANJUNG TOKONG

LEBUHRAYA FETTES 3

LEBUHRAYA FETTES 2

LEBUHRAYA FETTES 1

JALAN GAJAH

**PEPPER
ESTATE
(BUKIT LADA)**

JL FETTES

LINTANG FETTES

ORCHARD
AVENUE

GREENMIN
DRIVE

JALAN KERLING SANGKA

JL BUNGA
MELATI

JALAN SATRIA

JALAN EVERGREEN DRIVE

**FETTES
PARK**

JALAN BATU BUKIT

LR BATU
BUKIT

TAMAN TANJUNG 2

JALAN FETTES

GREENMIN DRIVE

PSR
HABLOR

NEWSPRING
DRIVE

LORONG BATU BUKIT 2

TAMAN TANJUNG 1

JALAN FETTES

M

JL FETTES

H DISC N DAT

LEBUH HALIA 1

LEBUHRAYA HALIA

PESIARAN LENGKUAS

PSR HALIA 1

LENGKOK HALIA

LENGKOK HALIA

CORONG HALIA

TINGKAT HALIA

JALAN TINGKUAS

PESIARAN LENGKUAS

JALAN TINGKUAS

LORONG LENGKUAS

TINGKAT LENGKUAS

EVERGREEN ROAD 4

EVERGREEN ROAD 5

Batu Ferringghi's Beach Resort Mile

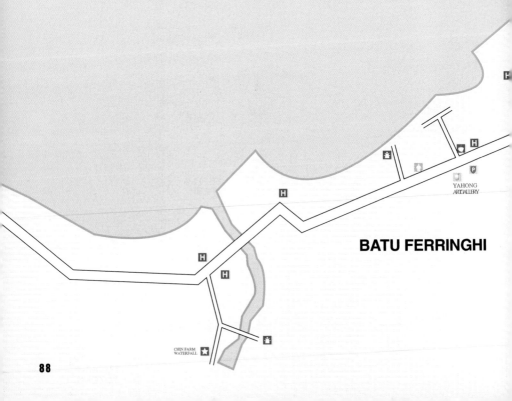

YAHONG ARTGALLERY

BATU FERRINGHI

CHIN FARM WATERFALL

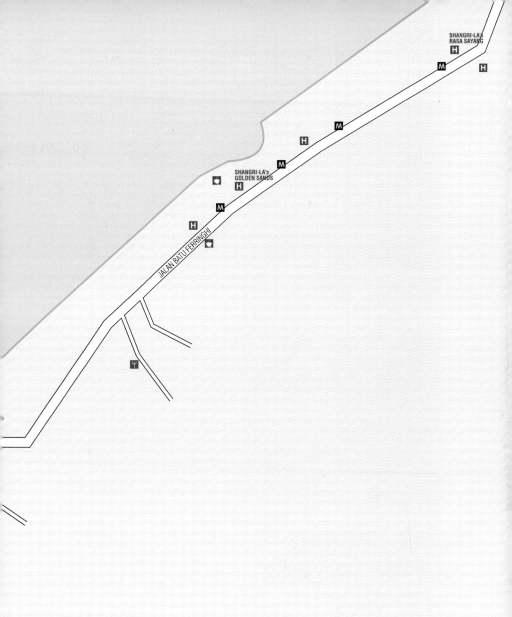

SHANGRI-LA's
RASA SAYANG

SHANGRI-LA's
GOLDEN SANDS

JALAN BATU FERRINGHI

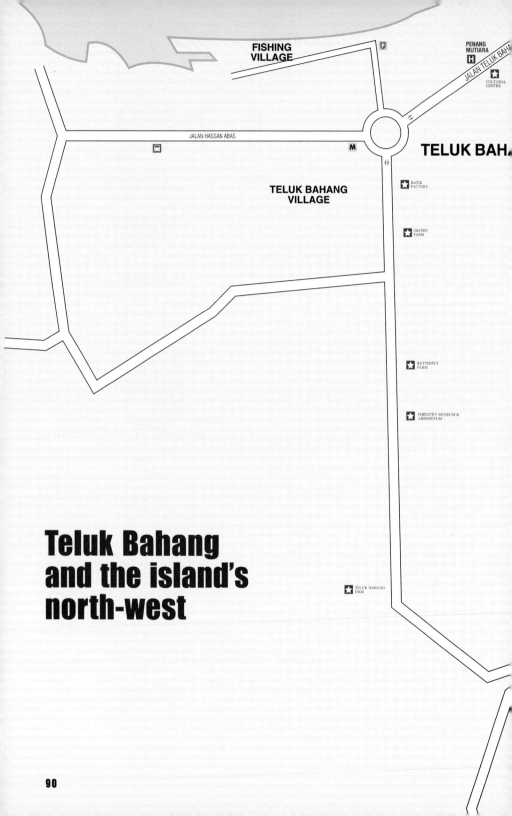

FISHING
VILLAGE

PENANG
MUTIARA

CULTURAL
CENTRE

JALAN HASSAN ABAS

TELUK BAH

TELUK BAHANG
VILLAGE

BATIK
FACTORY

ORCHID
FARM

BUTTERFLY
FARM

FORESTRY MUSEUM &
ARBORETUM

TELUK BAHANG
DAM

Teluk Bahang and the island's north-west

TheRealGuide's
Penang
Blue Pages

For over two hundred years, Penang has been attracting travellers to her shores. Her people are comfortable with visitors and her services and facilities continue to evolve to suit the changing needs of the over three million who visit from all over the world each year.

Chief among the island-hinterland state's new services and facilities for her visitors are the specialised medical care and retirement homes now available for the region. The rapid growth in the establishment of medical specialist centres in the state is the single, most significant change in what Penang has to offer the traveller today.

In addition, Penang has also been a regional education centre since the end of WW II. When the Malaysian government began promoting the growth of private colleges to meet the nation's higher education needs, this English-speaking state of Malaysia saw a blooming of institutions with course ties to universities in England, the United States and Australia.

The Blue Pages is designed to help you plan and budget for your stay in Penang.

Its three sections provide detailed information on product and/or service establishments in the state which have been independently checked out for quality and dependability by the publishers, a more comprehensive contact number only listing of such establishments, and, useful facts and language information to aid the visitor, respectively.

We trust you will find use for the information compiled in this section and wish you a very warm welcome to Penang.

Cititel Penang

66 Jalan Penang, 10000 Penang, Malaysia
Telephone : (60-4) 370 1188
Facsimile : (60-4) 370 2288
Email : infopen@cititelhotel.com
Internet : http://www.cititelhotel.com

Handbook Notes
Centrally located in the heart of Georgetown, along the famed Penang Road. Cititel Penang is just 5 minutes away from all Commercial and Government offices, 30 minutes from the Bayan Lepas International Airport and 5 minutes from the Ferry Terminal. Enjoy walking tours of the inner city and explore the historical sights of Penang!

Accommodation	Single	Double	Number
Standard	RM 175 *	RM 205 *	279
Superior	RM 215 *	RM 245 *	62
Corner	RM 260 *	RM 290 *	36
Superior Corner	RM 300 *	RM 330 *	8
Pinnacle Regular	RM 305 *	RM 375 *	58
Pinnacle Corner	RM 350 *	RM 420 *	4
Suite Room	RM 525 *	RM 525 *	4

* All rates are inclusive of 10% service charge and 5% government tax

Food & Beverage Outlets
24-hour Main Street Cafe - Local, Asian and International Cuisine
Fu Ling Men Chinese Restaurant - Cantonese & Szechuan Cuisine
Kirishima Japanese Restaurant - Authentic Japanese Cuisine
1st Avenue - Sports Bar & Lounge
Crystal KTV Karaoke Lounge - Karaoke Entertainment with Private Rooms

Amenities, Facilities & Services
A fully equipped Business Centre to offer an "office away from the office" convenience to business travellers, Rentable office suites for long or short term use with support secretarial and telephone services, Exclusive Pinnacle Floor (Executive Floor) for the discerning business traveller, Health Centre with steam, sauna and massage rooms, jacuzzi pool, medical service, organised tours, limousines, ticketing and self-drive cars, currency exchange, florist *Room Amenities and Services* - Air-conditioning with ceiling fans, Attached bathroom with long bath and shower, In-room fridge, Hairdryer, Coffee/Tea making facilities, Colour television, 24-hour Room Service, Laundry Service, Baby Cots, Satellite TV

Arcade
"The Mart" - The convenience store, located on the Lobby Level, houses a wide selection of gifts and souvenirs, books and magazines, minibar supplies and general sundries.

Office Suites
A unique feature of Cititel Penang is rentable office suites for long or short term use with support secretarial and telephone services

Credit Cards Accepted
American Express, Diners Club, JCB, MasterCard, Visa

CITITEL
Penang • Malaysia

Your Business-Friendly Hotel

Managed by Cititel Hotel Management Sdn. Bhd.

Conference & Banqueting (MICE) Facilities									
Level 3	Area (m²)	Banquet	Boardroom	Classroom	Cocktail	Hollow Square	Reception	Theatre	U-Shape
Perdana Ballroom*	632.50	500	190	420	750	190	750	850	170
Perdana I	90.75	60	36	45	80	36	80	90	30
Perdana II	90.75	60	36	45	80	36	80	90	30
Perdana III	189.75	160	60	110	200	70	200	270	60
Perdana IV	253.00	200	90	180	350	90	350	400	80
Bayan Room	92.00	70	36	45	80	36	80	90	30

* Comprises three demountable partitions to cater for space requirement of different seating capacities

The City Bayview Hotel, Penang

25-A Farquhar Street, 10200 Penang, Malaysia
Telephone : (60-4) 263 3161
Facsimile : (60-4) 263 4124
Email : cbvpg@tm.net.my

Handbook Notes
Ideally located in the heart of Georgetown to offer a perfect mix of business and leisure. Within easy walking distance to commercial, banking and shopping centres as well as the historical and cultural landmarks of Penang. 45 minutes away from the Bayan Lepas International Airport and just about 5 minutes from the ferry terminal.

Accommodation

Accommodation	Single	Double	Number
Superior (City View)	RM 280 *	RM 300 *	80
Deluxe (Heritage & Sea Views)	RM 330 *	RM 350 *	106
Grand Deluxe(Heritage View)	RM 380 *	RM 400 *	9
Junior Suite (Sea View)	RM 600 *	RM 600 *	10
Parlour Suite (Heritage View)	RM 1250 *	RM 1250 *	1
VIP Suite (Heritage View)	RM 1500 *	RM 1500 *	1
Presidential Suite	RM 2000 *	RM 2000 *	1

* Above rates are inclusive of daily breakfast, lunch and dinner.
* All rates are inclusive of 10% service charge and 5% government tax

Food & Beverage Outlets
Kopi Tiam (Level 1) - Serves buffet breakfast, local and colonial western fare in a refreshing ambience with a Mediterranean touch. Opens 7am - 1am daily.
Lobby Lounge (Level 1) - For cocktails, specially brewed coffee and other refreshments with entertainment. Opens 11am - 1am daily.
The Revolving Restaurant (Level P) - A novel way to dine. Enjoy its sunset buffet dinner at the one-and-only Revolving Restaurant with excellent views of the city. Opens 5pm - 12midnight (Sun - Fri) and 5pm - 1am (Sat and Eve of Public Holidays).
Carmen N.Y. Club (Basement) - A nightspot for the high-spirited, with live entertainment. Opens from 5pm - 2am (Sun - Thurs) and 5pm - 3am (weekends). Closed on Sundays.
Golden Lotus(Level 2) - Chinese Restaurant. Serves Cantonese and Szechuan dishes. Opens daily from 11.30am - 2.30pm and 6.30pm - 10.30pm.

Amenities, Facilities and Services
Fully equipped business centre with complete secretarial services as well as meeting rooms for small groups. Out-door free form swimming pool. Ballroom with capacity for 700 persons & 10 private meeting room. 24-hour room service. Executive floors, Ladies floor & non-smoking floor (upon request). Concierge. Laundry & dry cleaning. Tour arrangement. Baby sitting. Limousine & car rental. Safe deposit Box. Multi-storey parking. Daily Newspaper. Air Ticketing Service. Valet Service. Doctor on Call.
Room Amenities & Services - Guestrooms are designed to be spacious, with a home-away-from home coziness, as well as providing superb Heritage, Sea and/or City views. All rooms are well appointed with modern amenities expected of an international standard hotel. Special attention to details include separate shower cubicles in bathrooms. Air-conditioning with individual control. Pipe-in music. ASTRO Satellite TV channels. Mini bar. Hair dryer. Toilet Amenities. IDD telephone. Coffee/tea making facilities. Shaver outlet (110/240V). Bathrobe (for Suite-guests only). Bolster (for Suite-guests only).

Credit Cards Accepted
American Express, Diners Club, JCB, MasterCard, Visa

Whether your visit is for business or pleasure,
nothing compares to a more warm and friendly getaway.
Where else than at The City Bayview Hotel, Penang of course
... after all, we're in the heart of city!
Just call our Sales team at (60-4) 2633 161 ext. 207/208!

Regional Sales & Reservations Offices

Kuala Lumpur
Tel : (60-3) 2163 4899
Fax : (60-3) 2164 0632

Melbourne
Tel : (61-3) 9820 2222
Fax : (61-3) 9820 9586

United Kingdom
Tel : (44-1778) 342 288
Fax : (44-1778) 348 151

Singapore
Tel : (65) 339 1121 / 339 3077
Fax : (65) 339 3511
E-mail : bayintl@pacific.net.sg

Sydney
Tel : (61-2) 9357 2277
Fax : (61-2) 9356 2115

Conference & Banqueting (MICE) Facilities Level 4	Area (sq. ft.)	Sit Down	Theatre	U-Shape	Classroom	Buffet	Cocktail
Sri Mas Ballroom	6132	480	700	80	300	300	750
Sri Mas 1	2044	150	200	50	100	100	200
Sri Mas 2	2044	150	200	50	100	100	200
Sri Mas 3	2044	150	200	50	100	100	200
Sri Mas 1 & 2	4088	300	350	60	200	200	300
Sri Mas 2 & 3	4088	300	350	60	200	200	300
Sri Perak	2268	150	200	60	100	120	180
Sri Perak 1	756	50	60	24	33	40	60
Sri Perak 2	756	50	60	24	33	40	60
Sri Perak 3	756	50	60	24	33	40	60
Sri Perak 1 & 2	1512	100	120	50	66	80	120
Sri Perak 2 & 3	1512	100	120	50	66	80	120
Level 2							
Sri Nilam	1300	100	100	35	54	100	120
Sri Nilam 1	650	50	60	20	24	50	60
Sri Nilam 2	650	50	60	20	24	50	60
Sri Intan	650	40	60	20	24	40	60

Hotel Equatorial Penang

1 Jalan Bukit Jambul, Bayan Lepas, 11900 Penang, Malaysia
Telephone : (6 0-4) 643 8111
Facsimile : (6 0-4) 644 8000
E-mail : info@pen.equatorial.com
Website : http://www.equatorial.com

Handbook Notes

Perched on a hillock, the island's only golf and convention resort is strategically located 5 minutes (4km) away from the Bayan Lepas Industrial Zone, shopping mall, cineplex, banks and the Penang International Sports Arena; 10 minutes (8km) from the Penang International Airport; 25 minutes (15km) from the city centre; and is adjacent to the prestigious 18 hole Bukit Jambul Golf Course.

Accommodation	Single	Twin	Number
Superior	RM 483.00 *	RM 506.00 *	244
Deluxe	RM 529.00 *	RM 552.00 *	94
	(Above rates are inclusive of breakfast)		
Executive Deluxe	RM 552.00 *	RM 575.00 *	168
Equator Club Floor	RM 621.00 *	RM 644.00 *	62
Junior Suite	RM 805.00 *		8
Executive Suite	RM 989.00 *		24
Senator Suite	RM 1,472.00 *		7
Presidential Suite	RM 3,622.00 *		2

(Rates for suites are inclusive of Equator Club privileges)
(Two bedroom/one bedroom garden suite apartments are available, Extra beds are chargeable at RM57.50. Under the Hotel Equatorial Penang's Family Plan, there is no additional charge for children aged 18 and below when sharing parents' room with no extra bed required. Reservations are held till 1800 hours unless guaranteed by a credit card or a deposit.)
* All rates are quoted nett, inclusive of 10% service charge and 5% government tax, and are subject to change without notice
Check-in time: 2.00 pm   Check-out time: 12 noon

Food & Beverage Outlets

Coffee Garden - Offers local and western fare, and nightly themed buffets like Curry Night on Monday, Pasta Fiesta on Tuesday, Mongolian Barbecue on Wednesday, Mexican Delights on Thursday, Fisherman's Night on Friday, and Barbecue on Saturday. Open all day.
Golden Phoenix - Szechuan and Cantonese cuisine. Dim sum is available for lunch. Open daily for lunch and dinner.
The View - The hotel's signature restaurant serves provencale cuisine. Open daily for lunch and dinner from Monday to Friday. Saturday - dinner only. Sunday and public holidays - close.
Kampachi - Authentic Japanese cuisine. The Saturday and Sunday Buffet Lunch is highly recommended. Open daily for lunch and dinner.
Le Bistro - An open kitchen concept delicatessen featuring pastas, salads, pastries and a selection of French country dishes.
Passe Temps - A cozy, quiet wine bar.
Blue Moon - enjoy classic island concoctions over entertainment from the live band, sports events on TV or in a casual game of pool or darts. Open every evening.
Room service: available all day

Amenities, Facilities and Services

Business Centre with internet and e-mail facilities, designated floors for non-smokers, medical clinic, Equator Club Floor, Japanese Floor, baby-sitting, express laundry and valet, car jockey services, covered carpark, tour & travel desk, limousine and taxi service, drugstore, currency exchange, scheduled complimentary shuttle service to airport, city centre and nearby shopping mall. *Room Amenities* - high-speed internet access, satellite radio and television (English and Japanese), IDD telephone with bathroom extension, 2 IDD lines in deluxe rooms/ suites and Executive Wing rooms, direct inward dialing, keycard lock system, voice mail system, individually programmed wake-up call, mini-bar, tea and coffee making facilities, in-room electronic safe, hairdryer, longbath with shower, longbath with individual cubicle shower in deluxe rooms and suites, daily local newspaper, individual balcony *Recreational Facilities* - equipped Fitness Centre with weights room, aerobics studio and separate male/female facilities for sauna, steambath and jacuzzi, reflexology, massage, beauty and health treatments using aroma-therapeutic products, spa, reflexology path, squash and tennis (floodlit) courts, jogging tracks, outdoor swimming pool with jacuzzi and waterfall, driving range, putting green and teambuilding park.

Credit Cards Accepted

American Express, Diners Club, JCB, MasterCard, Visa

MICE Facilities

Recipient of the Prestige Publications' Excellence Award for Best Resort & Conventions in the Asia Pacific Region, the Hotel Equatorial Penang has played host to gatherings and functions of all types.

The hotel's unique ambience and convenient location has made it the top choice among heads-of-state, businessmen visiting Penang as well as conference and function planners. The hotel boasts the two largest column free ballrooms on the island:- the Matahari and Grand Ballrooms which can accommodate up to 1800 and 1500 people theatre style respectively. There are 21 other well-appointed function rooms which can host groups of 40 to 300 with ease, and an exhibition hall which can place 240 booths.

The function rooms are fully equipped with modern facilities which include high speed internet access, multi-translation system, barco vision and liquid crystal panel and white light projector.

(Please contact the Hotel Equatorial Penang for its full lay-out plan, and the seating capacities of its various function rooms).

Regional Sales Offices
Singapore Tel: (65) 333 5788 Fax: (65) 333 5766 Toll Free: 800-601 1800 **Kuala Lumpur** Tel: (60-3) 201 3030 Fax: (60-3) 201 1123
Toll Free: 1800- 88 1800 **Hong Kong** Tel: (852) 2368 1922 Fax: (852) 2366 7621 **United Kongdom** Tel: (44-1959) 525 113 Fax: (44-1959) 525 113
Japan Tel: (81-3) 5460 8021 Fax: (81-3) 5460 8050 **China** Tel: (86-21) 6210 0889 Fax: (86-21) 6210 0887
Thailand Tel: (66-2) 541 1234 Fax: (66-2) 541 1121
GDS (Use Vendor code NT to access Equatorial hotels) Amadeus/System One, Sabre/Axess, Galileo/Apollo, Worldspan/Abacus
A Member of Pegasus Commission Processing

Evergreen Laurel Hotel Penang

53 Persiaran Gurney, 10250 Penang, Malaysia
Telephone : (60-4) 226 9988
Facsimile : (60-4) 226 9989

Kuala Lumpur Sales Office
Suite 1205 (12th Fl) Kenaga International
Jalan Sultan Ismail
50250 Kuala Lumpur
Telephone : (60-3) 2166 1898
Facsimile : (60-3) 2166 1899

Food & Beverage Outlets

Café Laurel - Located on Lobby Floor. Serves a mix of local and western fare. Glass-fronted to provide superb view of Gurney Drive seafront. Seating capacity for 230 diners. Open from 6am to 1am daily. Daily buffet breakfasts. Daily buffet lunches on weekdays. Theme buffet dinners on Fridays to Sundays. High Tea buffets on weekends.

Canton Palace - Located on Level 1. Signature restaurant with seating capacity for 280 diners. Open for lunch and dinner daily, including Sundays and Public Holidays. Serves DimSum lunches and has an a-la-carte menu featuring Cantonese cuisine as well as an impressive selection of cocktails, wines and liquors. 8 private function rooms with TV entertainment and seating capacities for, from 16 to 24 diners. Emperor and Empress Private Rooms also include private washroom.

Lobby Lounge - Live band performance nightly. Happy Hours Daily from 5pm - 9pm with slash of 50% on standard pouring drinks and beer prices. Includes island bar which can seat 18.

Handbook Notes

Located along the scenic Gurney Drive seafront. Situated a walking distance from Penang's well-known hawker food centres there. A 3-minute drive from the city's business district, historic spots and shopping centres 25-30 minutes away from the Bayan Lepas Inrternational Airport and just 15 minutes from the island's famed Batu Feringghi beaches.

Accommodation	Rate	Number
Superior	RM 220 *	182
Deluxe	RM 250 *	182
Executive Suite	RM 360 *	9
Deluxe Suite	RM 970 *	2
Evergreen Suite	RM 1955 *	1

* All rates are inclusive of 10% service charge and 5% government tax
All Rooms: Personal Electronic Safe - Mini Bar - Newspaper - Coffee-and Tea-making facilities - Hairdryer & wall-mounted telephone in bathroom - colourTV with Astro channels

Amenities, Facilities and Services

Evergreen Laurel Health Club - Takes up entire second floor of hotel. Fully equipped gymnasium, Aerobics room, Swimming pool, Finnish saunas*, Steambaths*, Hot & Cold jacuzzis*, Massage**, 2 tennis courts**, Pool room**
Other Amenities, Facilities & Services - Fireproof and soundproof walls, Ice-pantry on each floor for complimentary guest use, Business Centre, Baggage Room, Gift Shop, Laundry & Valet, Hair & Beauty Salon, Hotel Shuttle Service

* Separate facilities for male & female guests
** Chargeable

Credit Cards Accepted

American Express, Diners Club, JCB, MasterCard, Visa

The Evergreen Laurel Hotel
"... simply the best"

Conference & Banqueting (MICE) Facilities

Level 1	Area (m²)	Banquet	Boardroom	Classroom	Cocktail	Hollow Square	Reception	Theatre	U-shape
Laurel 1	500	250	-	155	350	-	300	300	60
Laurel 2	360	150	-	90	200	-	200	200	40
Laurel 1 + 2	860	550	-	265	750	-	600	600	100

Penang Mutiara Beach Resort

1 Jalan Teluk Bahang, 11050 Penang, Malaysia
Telephone : (60-4) 885 2828
Facsimile : (60-4) 885 2829
Email : pmr@po.jaring.my
Web page : http://www.penang-mutiara.com.my

Handbook Notes

Located on prime beachfront at Teluk Bahang, also known as the 'glowing bay', Penang Mutiara is just 30 minutes away from the city centre and 45 minutes drive from the Bayan Lepas International Airport.

Accommodation	Rate		Number
Superior (Garden View)	RM	650 *	87
Deluxe (Sea-facing)	RM	740 *	171
Grande Deluxe (Sea View)	RM	830 *	146
Marina Studio	RM	960 *	51
Pelangi Executive Suite	RM	1680 *	21
Mutiara Suite	RM	2130 *	4
Mandarin Suite	RM	2800 *	1
Mandarin Suite (with Roof Garden)	RM	5040 *	5
Royal Suite (incl. Butler & limousine service)	RM	8400 *	1

Extra Bed (Rollaway) - RM 60 *

* All rates are inclusive of 10% service charge and 5% government tax (All rates are commissionable at 10% on base rate to all bona fide travel agents)

Food & Beverage Outlets

Garden Terrace Restaurant (24 hours) - For fine Local and International Cuisine
La Farfalla Italian Restaurant - Award-winning restaurant. Specialises in fine Italian dishes prepared in new wave style.
House Of Four Seasons Chinese Restaurant - Provides authentic Cantonese and Szechuan dishes.
Tsuru-No-Ya Japanese Restaurant - Serves traditional Japanese food
Palmetto Lounge- A great rendezvous where evenings come alive with music from a live band. Open daily from 11.00 am - 1.00am
Puppetry Lounge - Perfect for pre-dinner cocktails or after dinner drinks. Opens nightly from 6.00pm - 12.00am (except Mondays)

Amenities, Facilities and Services

Fully equipped business centre with complete secretarial services, 2 reflecting pools, Pool bar with stools semi-immersed in the swimming pools, Roof-top garden to hold cocktail funtions, Children's indoor and outdoor play area including Sinbad Kids Adventure Club, newly refurbished Ballroom with capacity for 800 persons & 5 private meeting rooms and additional meeting venue by the sea (the first in Penang), Recreation Centre with comprehensive range of activities for adults and children, Fitness Centre with a fully equipped gymnasium, steam and sauna baths, hot and cold whirlpools and massage services . Three tennis courts, one multipurpose court, squash courts and beachfront

Amenities, Facilities and Services (cont'd)

volleyball court, excellent Seasport & Watersports facilities, Marine Adventure 9-hole Mini Golf, Suites with rooftop gardens, Laundry and valet services, Concierge services, Airport Representatives
Room Amenities - Spacious balcony facing the sea, Wardrobe accessible from bathroom & bedroom, Colour television, IDD telephone with bathroom extension, Air-conditioning with individual controls, Ceiling fan, Fully stocked refrigerator in Suites, Complimentary coffee and tea making facility, Wall-to wall parquet "Permagrain" floor, Radio / TV with bedside controls, Hairdryer, Safe deposit box, Separate shower stall / WC Compartment, Twin wash basin, Long bath, Bidet in Exclusive Suites, Bathrobe, Electricity: 110/220 Volts

Arcade

Mutiara Trend, Drug Store, De Silva, Tailors, Art Gallery,Cherita Gift Shop, Hair & Beauty Private Collection, Le Chocolatier, Clinic

Credit Cards Accepted

American Express, Diners Club, JCB, MasterCard, Visa

Penang Mutiara is a perfect description of an extraordinary resort with a lively Malaysian hospitality. Being the only member of the Leading Hotels of The World In Penang, the resort has a range of exciting Promotions specially designed for you.

Just call our reservations Team at (604) 885 2828 extn: 324!

Regional Sales Offices

Japan/Korea	**Europe**
Tel : (813) 3663 1023	Tel : (44-1491) 637 537
Fax : (813) 3663 1024	Fax : (44-1491) 636 159
China/Hong Kong/Taiwan	**North America** **South Africa (GSA)**
Tel : (852) 2735 3222	Tel : (714) 228 0488 Tel : (27-11) 791 0300
Fax : (852) 2735 2889	Fax : (714) 228 0883 Fax : (27-11) 791 0052
Australia/New Zealand	**Singapore / Indonesia / Philippines /Thailand**
Sydney Office	Tel : (65) 235 8588
Tel : (612) 9255 7960	Fax : (65) 235 4588
Fax : (612) 9255 7962	**Malaysia/Brunei**
Melbourne Office	Tel : (60-3) 245 8823
Tel : (61-3) 9597 0979	Fax : (60-3) 243 0823
Fax : (61-3) 9579 0990	

Conference & Banqueting (MICE) Facilities

Lobby (West Wing)	Area (m²)	Banquet	Boardroom	Classroom	Cocktail	Hollow Square	Theatre	U-shape
Mutiara Ballroom	607.20	550	102	350	600	-	800	-
Banquet Room Atrina	166.52	100	34	100	120	40	150	40
Banquet Room Bursa	274.17	150	34	140	250	55	240	55
Banquet Room Cassis	166.52	100	34	100	120	40	150	40
Ballroom Foyer	210.60	-	-	-	-	-	-	-
Floor 5 Meeting Rooms								
Captain Room 1 (Diloma)	56.34	20	20	25	50	20	50	40
Captain Room 2 (Ecmanis)	56.34	20	20	25	50	20	50	40
Captain Room 3 (Fulvia)	56.34	20	20	25	50	20	50	40
Captain Room 4 (Gadila)	56.34	20	20	25	50	20	50	40
Captain Room 5 (Hermes)	56.34	20	20	25	50	20	50	40

Shangri-La Hotel Penang

Jalan Magazine, 10300 Penang, Malaysia
Telephone : (60-4) 262 2622
Facsimile : (60-4) 262 6526
Email : slp@shangri-la.com
Web page : http://www.shangri-la.com

Shangri-La hotel

PENANG, MALAYSIA

Handbook Notes
Located just next to Penang's transport hub at KOMTAR (on the Jalan Magazine side) the Shangri-La Hotel Penang is well-placed for those who need ready access to transportation services when on their stay here. Positioned for the business traveller, the Hotel is also favoured by the out-of-town visitor who prefer city conveniences.

Accommodation	Single	Double	Number
Superior	RM 437 *	RM 460 *	108
Deluxe	RM 460 *	RM 483 *	293
Horizon Club	RM 552 *	RM 575 *	29
	Single[1]	Double[2]	Number
Executive Suite	RM 805 *	RM 1150 *	12
Pinang Suite	RM 1380 *	RM 1840 *	1
Horizon Suite	RM 1725 *	RM 2070 *	1
Malaysian Suite	RM 1955 *	RM 2530 *	1

[1] 1 BdRM   [2] 2 BdRM
* All rates are inclusive of 10% service charge and 5% government tax
Horizon Club - Exclusive executive floor, with private lounge for breakfast and cocktails in the evenings

Food & Beverage Outlets
Coffee Garden (24 hours) - Local and International Cuisine
The Brasserie - Continental Cuisine. Open daily. Lunch (12.00pm - 2.30pm) and Dinner (7.00pm - 10.30pm)
Shang Palace - Chinese & Hong Kong Dim Sum. Open daily. Lunch (11.30am - 2.30pm) and Dinner (6.30pm - 10.00pm)
Desperado's - Music Bar & Live Band Performance. Open daily except Sundays. Monday - Wednesday (6.00pm - 1.00am) and (Thursday - Saturday) 6.00pm -2.00am)
Lobby Lounge - Lounge Music. Open daily from 10am - 12am)

Amenities, Facilities and Services
Fully equipped business centre with complete secretarial services. Laundry and valet, baby-sitting service, Hair Salon, Facilities for the handicapped. Schedule shuttle bus service to sister properties at Batu Feringgi (Rasa Sayang & Golden Sands Resorts) including Inter-signing and Use of Facilities there,

Amenities, Facilities and Services (cont'd)
Limousine, Car Rental, Drugstore & Tour Desk. *Recreation* - Outdoor swimming pool, with children's pool. Fitness Centre with fully equipped gymnasium, sauna, steam bath and massage services.

Credit Cards Accepted
American Express, Diners Club, JCB, MasterCard, Visa

Meetings & Conventions
Centrally located in the heart of George Town, Shangri-La Hotel Penang offers a variety of choices for your meetings and conventions.
Theme Events - We specialize in organizing theme parties and meetings, including *Penang Chinatown, Colonial Nights, Safari Adventure, Kampung Ku* and *Masquerade Party*.
Heritage Sites - Outside catering for theme events can be arranged at Penang's famous heritage sites including *Khoo Kongsi, Cheong Fatt Tze Mansion, Cheah Kongsi* and *Convent Light Street*.

Banquets and Conference
A grand ballroom with additional 7 smaller meeting rooms, with a capacity for banquet functions ranging from 60 - 800 persons. Fully equipped with the latest audio-visual equipment and a wide range of conference facilities.

Room	Area (m²)	Reception	Theatre	Banquet	Classroom	U-shape	
Pinang Ballroom	482	350	600	400	250	100	(Single)
Pinang 1	241	150	270	160	120	55	(Single)
Pinang I	241	150	270	160	120	55	(Single)
Pinang Foyer	265	100	180	150	50	35	
Tioman Room	164	70	100	130	63	N/A	
Rawa Room	63	30	50	50	18	20	
Redang Room	50	20	40	16	15	16	
Rimau Room	50	20	40	40	16	15	
Pinang Ballroom & Foyer		450	800	620	300		
Pinang Ballroom & Foyer & Tioman Room		700	1100	850	350		
Pangkor Room	119	50	120	100	70	35	
Pangkor I	59	20	50	40	27	17	
Pangkor II	59	20	50	40	27	17	
Langkawi Room	119	50	120	100	70	35	
Langkawi Room I	59	20	50	40	27	17	
Langkawi Room II	59	20	50	40	27	17	

Shangri-La's Golden Sands Resort

Batu Feringgi Beach
11100 Penang
Telephone : (604) 881 1911
Facsimile : (604) 881 1880
Web page : http://www.shangri-la.com

Shangri-La's

Rasa Sayang Resort Golden Sands Resort
PENANG, MALAYSIA

Handbook Notes
Located on the beach front at Batu Feringgi on the north-west coast of Penang Island. Set on Penang's most popular beach, the resort is 17 kms (20 minutes) from Georgetown and 31 kms (45 minutes) from the Penang International Airport.

Accommodation	Single	Double
Island View	RM 340 *	RM 400 *
Garden View	RM 420 *	RM 480 *
Seaview Room	RM 520 *	RM 580 *
Deluxe Seaview	RM 570 *	RM 630 *
Executive Suite	RM 1,250 *	RM 1,250 *

Extra Bed - RM 60.00 *

Food & Beverage Outlets
Garden Café - Located across the lobby, overlooking the garden. Open-air, casual with tropical setting. Smoking and non-smoking sections. 24-hour operations serving international and local food.
Peppino - Located at the lobby level, next to the reception counter, overlooking the garden. Italian style décor and setting, air-conditioned with smoking and non-smoking sections. Pizza show kitchen and a service bar. Open daily for dinner only.
"Sigi's by the Sea" Bistro-Bar - Located at the beach front. Bistro-bar, colorful, fun, casual open-air dining with alfresco based menu and a cocktail bar. Open daily for continental breakfast and dinner.
Kuda Laut - Located at the poolside garden. Tropical setting with poolbar and restaurant accompanied by parasol settings. Open daily from 10.30am to 7.30pm.
Sunset Lounge - Located at the lobby level. Casual, open air, overlooking the garden. Open daily from 10.30am to 1.00am.

Room Service available 24 hours

Amenities, Facilities & Services
Baby-sitting services, clinic, complimentary scheduled shuttle service between resort and city, cross-signing facilities at sister hotels and resorts, drugstore, Starfy Star Kids Club, hair and beauty salon, limousine and car rental service, same-day laundry and valet service, self service launderette, shopping arcade, tour and travel office.

Recreation - Swimming pool, tennis court, non-motorised watersports facilities, massage, multi purpose court, trapeze, archery, and trampoline.

Mini Gymnasium - Located at the beachfront and next to Garden Cafe. State-of-the-art equipment. Opening hours from 7.00am to 9.00pm.

Conference & Banqueting Services
Offer two main function rooms which can be divided into six small meeting rooms. Can accomodate from 18 to 400 people. Meeting packages available.

Shangri-La's Rasa Sayang Resort

Batu Feringgi Beach, 11100 Penang, Malaysia
Telephone : (60-4) 881 1811
Facsimile : (60-4) 881 1984 / 881 2759

Handbook Notes
Located on the beach front at Batu Feringgi on the north-west coast of Penang Island. Set on Penang's finest beach, the resort is 17 km or 20 mins drive from Georgetown and 31 kms or 45 mins from the Penang International Airport.

Accommodation	Single	Twin
Main Wing		
Standard	RM 490 *	RM 550 *
Seafacing	RM 600 *	RM 660 *
Deluxe Seafacing	RM 700 *	RM 760 *

Accommodation	Single	Twin
Executive Suite	RM 1,000	RM 1,000
Tranquil Suite[3]	RM 4,500	

[1] 1 BdRM - 5th Floor [2] 1 BdRm - 4th Floor [3] 2 BdRm - 4th & 5th Floor

Garden Wing		
Deluxe Seafacing	RM 700 *	RM 760 *
Parlour Suite	RM 1,000 *	RM 1,000 *
Studio Suite	RM 1,500 *	RM 1,500 *
Terrace Suite	RM 2,500 *	RM 2,500 *
Master Suite	RM 3,500 *	RM 3,500 *

Extra Bed - RM 60 *
* For both resorts, all rates quoted are inclusive of Service Charge and Government Tax. The rates quoted are valid until December 19, 2000. For reservations after dates mentioned, please call the resort's Reservation Department. Shangri-La's Family Plan provides children (to the maximum of 1) up to 18 years of age with free accommodation when staying in the same room as their parents. Should more than one room be required to accommodate your family, each room will be made available at the single room rate. For every one parent paying for a buffet breakfast or buffet

Accommodation - Beach, City, Hill Hotels & Resorts

dinner, one child 6 years or younger will be entitled for the same meal without charge. Additional child(ren) will be charged 50% off that buffet prices.

Check-in time: 2.00pm Check-out time: 12.00 noon

Food & Beverage Outlets

Ferringhi Grill - Located at ground floor, Main Wing. Resort's premier restaurant for champagne and chablis, and excellent continental cuisine. Feringgi Bar attached for before-, and after-dinner drinks. Open for dinner. Reservations are recommended.

Waka - Finest Japanese Restaurant in town. Popular with locals for its sumptous buffet dinner on Wednesday and Friday plus Sunday brunch. A-la-carte menu available. Located at garden wing. Reservations recommended. Open for dinner except Sunday.

Shang Court - Serving fine Cantonese cuisine. Acclaimed by locals for its buffet dinner on Tuesday and Saturday plus Sunday brunch. Live entertainment on Saturday. A-la-carte menu with 100 different dishes. Open for dinner except Sunday.

Coffee Garden - Open from 7.00am to 1.00am. Partially open-air coffee shop. Serves buffet breakfast and wide selection of local and international dishes. Situated at Main Wing.

Garden Terrace - Open for breakfast daily. Located at Garden Wing. Serving international and local dishes in a light airy buffet presentation.

Lobby Lounge - A gathering point for drinks, light snacks and evening entertainment by a live band. Located at Main Wing. Open from 11:00am to 12:45am daily.

Tepi Laut - Sits snugly on the seafront. A place to quench tropical thirsts and savour light snacks. Under-the-stars dining every Tuesday, Thursday, Friday and Saturday (weather permitting). Open from 10:30am to 11:00pm.

The Pool Bar - Located at Garden Wing. Stands by the beach against a tropical garden. An oasis for tall ice-cold cocktails, casual lunches and light dinner. Open from 11:00am to 10pm.

Room service available 24 hours.

Amenities, Facilities and Services

Business Centre with meeting rooms (equipped with a wide range of state-of-the-art conference and audio-visual equipment), facsimile, telex, photocopier, courier, secretarial services, and personal computers for guest use, same day laundry & valet service, baby-sitting service, limousine & car rental service, Starfy's Star Kids Club, 4 swimming pools inclusive of children's pool, unique tree house and slide, Health Club, 3 tennis courts, table tennis, sailing, boating, water skiing, daily organised recreational and social activities, and cross signing privileges at sister hotels and resorts in Penang   ***Room Amenities & Services*** - Colour TV with satellite programmes and in-house movies, IDD telephone, fully stocked mini-bar, bathroom with telephone and radio speaker, tea and coffee-making facilities, in-room safe and hairdryer ***Arcade*** - Hair and beauty salon, Gift Shop, Florist, Boutiques, Pro-Golf Shop, Antiques.

Conference & Banqueting Facilities

The Pelangi Ballroom can accomodate up to 500 people for a sit down dinner and a choice of 7 function rooms which can break-up into 16 meeting rooms. Two permanent boardrooms are ready with the state-of-the-art audio-visual equipment with capability to have 10 people meeting in comfort. All conference and meeting rooms are equipped with a wide range of state-of-the-art conference and audio-visual equipment.

Theme dinners and meeting packages available for those who like to work and enjoy at the same place. Team building village is also available for corporate citizens to test their skills and enhance teamwork spirit.

Credit Cards Accepted (for both Resorts)

American Express, Diners Club, JCB, MasterCard, Visa

Worldwide Sales & Reservations

For reservations at any Shangri-La or Traders Hotel, call your travel consultant or the nearest Shangri-La or Traders Hotel

AUSTRALIA (Toll-free: (1-800) 222 448 (Sydney: (61-2) 9262 2588) CANADA (Toll-free: (1-800) 942 5050) DENMARK (Toll-free: (800) 181 73) FINLAND (Toll-free: (0-800) 908 687) FRANCE (Toll-Free: (0-800) 908 687 GERMANY (Toll-free: (0-130) 856 649 HONG KONG: (85-2) 2331 6688) INDONESIA (Jakarta: (62-21) 570 7445) JAPAN (Tokyo: (81-3) 3263 7071) MALAYSIA (Toll-free: (1-800) 88 3778) NEW ZEALAND (Toll-free: (0-800) 442 179) NORWAY (Toll-free: (800) 11 779) SINGAPORE: (65) 535 3578) SWEDEN (Toll-free: (020) 795 171) SWITZERLAND (Toll-free: (0-800) 556 333) TAIWAN (Taipei: 1866-2 2378 8888) THAILAND (Bangkok: (66-2) 236 7777) UNITED KINGDOM (London: 44-181) 747 8485) UNITED STATES (Toll-free: (1-800) 942 5050 (Los Angeles: (1-310) 665 2000 (New York: (1-212) 768 3190)

Sunway Hotel Penang

33 New Lane, 10400 Penang, Malaysia
Telephone : (60-4) 229 9988
Facsimile : (60-4) 228 8899
Email : sunway@swhtlpg.po.my

Handbook Notes
Centrally located in historical, bustling Georgetown, right in the heart of the island where both culture and commerce dwell at its best. The Sunway hotel is within easy walking distance to one of Penang's famous landmarks, KOMTAR, the hub of government activities which also houses Penang's largest shopping complex.

Accommodation	Single	Double			Number	
Superior	RM 280 *	RM 300 *			14[1]	46[2]
Deluxe	RM 310 *	RM 330 *			64[1]	101[2]
Executive	RM 350 *	RM 370 *			11[1]	
Sri Rambai Suite	RM 470 *	RM 490 *			5[1]	
Marquis Cornwallis Suite	RM 570 *	RM 590 *			2[1]	

[1] King Bed [2] Twin
* All rates are inclusive of 10% service charge and 5% government tax.

Food & Beverage Outlets
"Tropics" Cafe - Serves a variety of reknowned Penang and International specialities (160 seats)
Nutmegs - Lobby lounge offers a more casual and relaxed atmosphere. Refreshing beverages and food are served throughout the day.

Amenities, Facilities and Services
Business Centre at the lobby level provides the executive guest with administrative services e.g. fax, secretarial support, translations, internet access and personal computers. Swimming pool with jacuzzi. Fully equipped gymnasium. Travel arrangements. Laundry and valet service. Safe deposit boxes. Indoor car park. Baby-sitting service. *Room Amenities & Services* - Individually controlled air-conditioning. Oversized beds. Colour TV with satellite programmes. Radio. IDD Telephone. Mini-bar. Complimentary tea/coffee facilities. Large working desk. Hairdryer. 24-hour In-Room Dining. *Arranged Services* - Tennis, Squash, Sauna and Massage

Credit Cards Accepted
American Express, Diners Club, JCB, MasterCard, Visa

Worldwide Sales & Reservations
For reservations please contact your professional travel planner, Summit International Hotels, Allson International Sales Offices, or, any Allson or Sunway Hotel directly
Kuala Lumpur Sales Office
Level 15 Sunway Lagoon Resort, Persiaran Lagoon, Bandar Sunway, 46150 Petaling Jaya, Selangor Dahrul Ehsan, Malaysia.
Tel: (60-3) 731 6077   Fax: (60-3) 731 6197
ASIA   Hong Kong Tel: (85-2) 2866 8369 Fax: (85-2) 2529 0756
Singapore Tel: (65) 339 4048 Fax: (65) 339 4482   Kuala Lumpur Tel: (60-3) 731 6077 Fax: (60-3) 731 6197)   Paris - France Tel: (33 - 1) 4421 8058 Fax: (33 - 1) 4421 4057   London - United Kingdom Tel: (44 - 171) 242 9966 Fax: (44 - 171) 242 2838   Milan - Italy Tel: (39 - 2) 3310 5838 Fax: (39 - 2) 3310 5827

Worldwide Sales & Reservations (cont'd)
Allson International Hotels & Resorts (Corporate Office)
2410 Dominion Centre, 45-59 Queen's Road East, Wanchai, Hong Kong
Tel: (85 - 2) 2866 8350   Fax: (85 - 2) 2529 0756
Email: aihrhk@netvigator.com
Corporate Sales & Marketing and Regional Office
Sunway Lagoon Resort Hotel, Persiaran Lagoon, Bandar Sunway, 46150 Petaling Jaya, Selangor Darul Ehsan, Malaysia
Tel: (60 - 3) 7492 5222   Fax: (60 - 3) 7492 0636
Email: allson@po.jaring.my
Internet: http://www.allsonhotels.com.my/allson or www.allsonhotels.com

Allson Operated Hotels
Allson Residence - Mitra Oasis, Jakarta, Indonesia
Allson Hotel, Singapore
Allson Genesis Hotel, Bukit Bintang, Kuala Lumpur
Allson Klana, Bandar Baru Nilai, Malaysia
Allson Klana Resort, Seremban, Malaysia
Sunway Hotel, Phnom Penh, Cambodia
Sunway Hotel, Hanoi, Vietnam
Sunway Hotel, George Town, Malaysia
Sunway Hotel, Seberang Jaya, Penang, Malaysia
Sunway Lagoon Resort Hotel, Petaling Jaya, Malaysia
Hotels under Development
Kuala Lumpur, Malaysia (2001)

An Ⓐ *ALLSON INTERNATIONAL HOTEL*
Owned by Sunway City Berhad
(A member of The SunwayGroup)

Conference* & Banqueting** (MICE)Facilities

Venue	Area (m²)	Banquet	Boardroom	Classroom	Cocktail	Hollow Square	Reception	Theatre	U-Shape
Bougainvillaea	114	70	30	50	80	-	80	100	30
Hibiscus	114	70	30	80	80	-	80	100	30
Dahlia	111	70	30	35	50	-	80	60	26

Casuarina Beach Resort Penang

Batu Ferringhi, 11100 Penang, Malaysia
Telephone : (60-4) 881 1711
Facsimile : (60-4) 881 2155
Email : caspen@tm.net.my
Internet : http://www.casuarina.com.my
Telex : CASPEN MA40137
Toll-Free : (1-800) 88 8255 (Malaysia only)

Handbook Notes
Fringing the shores of Penang's famed Batu Ferringhi beach, the Casuarina Beach Resort pervades with the warmth of Penang hospitality.This cozy 180-room resort successfully blends nature's charms with modern comforts.

Accommodation

	Single	Double
Deluxe	RM 400 *	RM 420 *

Extra Bed - RM 70* each   Baby Cot - RM 30* each
* Rates are nett & inclusive of 10% service and 5% government tax.

Food & Beverage Outlets
Il Ritrovo - a delightfully cosy restaurant offering choice Italian cuisine and fine wines
Garden Terrace - casual dining, local and continental fare
Pool Bar - drinks and snacks by the pool
Asmara Lounge - live band entertainment and drinks

Amenities, Facilities and Services
Swimming pool, Drugstore, Limousine and car rental, Safe deposit boxes, Tennis court, Table tennis, Hairdressing salon, Laundry, 24-hour room service, Doctor on call, Foreign exchange, Baby-sitting, Organised guest activities
Room Amenities & Services - Private balcony, Private bath, Shower, Piped-in music, Minibar, Colour television with access to satellite channels and in-house movies, Air-conditioning, IDD telephone, Coffee/tea-making facilities, Hairdryer

Credit Cards Accepted
American Express, Diners Club, MasterCard, Visa

Conference & Banqueting (MICE) Facilities

Level 2 Theatre	Area (sq ft) U-Shape	Banquet	Boardroom	Classroom	Cocktail	Hollow Square		Reception	
Tanjung Bunga Room	1,440	100	40	40	100	30	100	60	30

Copthorne Orchid Penang

Tanjung Bungah, 11200 Penang, Malaysia
Telephone : (60-4) 890 3333
Facsimile : (60-4) 890 3303
Email : copenexec@po.jaring.my

Handbook Notes
Situated on a private seafront with an excellent view of the Tanjung Bungah Bay is one of the nearest hotels to the City of Georgetown and the International Airport.

Accommodation

	Single/Double	Number
Superior	RM 270 *	100
Deluxe (Tower)	RM 300 *	146
Deluxe (Terrace)	RM 330 *	28
Junior Suite (Tower)	RM 370 *	24
Junior Suite (Terrace)	RM 400 *	14
Executive Suite	RM 800 *	5
Presidential Suite	RM 3,500 *	1

Extra bed - RM 50*
Baby Cot - Complimentary
* All rates are inclusive of 10% service and 5% government tax.
Special monthly rates are available upon request

Food & Beverage Outlets
Terrace Bay - Local and International delicacies
Hua Ting Chinese Restaurant - Serves exquisite Cantonese and Szechuan cuisine and popular dim sum delicacies.
Lobby Lounge - Offers refreshing cocktails.
STARS Karaoke - For a relaxing evening

SHOCK Egypt Discotheque - The heartbeat of Penang. **Amenities, Facilities and Services** Business and Internet Centre. Complimentary scheduled shuttle service, same day laundry and valet service, baby-sitting services, children's playground, swimming pool and children pool, recreation centre with sauna, massage, jacuzzi and fully equipped gymnasium, squash courts, and nearby tennis court. Indoor carpark, currency exchange, drug store and hair salon. **Room Amenities & Services** - All rooms with private balcony, individually controlled air-conditioning, direct dial telephone and personal bar. Colour TV with satellite programs complimented with in-house movies. 24-hour room service, tea and coffee-making facilities, in-room safe, hairdryer, iron and ironing board (upon request)

Credit Cards Accepted
American Express, Diners Club, JCB, MasterCard, Visa.

Conference & Banqueting Facilities
Penang Ballroom with maximum capacity of 600 theatre-style, 300 classroom and 550 banqueting and 5 other well-designed function rooms.

Paradise Sandy Bay - Penang

527 Jalan Tanjung Bungah, 11200 Penang, Malaysia
Telephone : (60-4) 899 9999
Facsimile : (60-4) 899 0000
E-Mail : sandybay@po.jaring.my
Web page : http://www.paradisehotel.com

Handbook Notes
Located at the Tanjung Bungah beachfront area. Central location that gets you to just about anywhere easily in minutes. Only 40 minutes away from the airport and a 45-minute flight from the Kuala Lumpur International Airport.

Accommodation	Rate	Number
Studio	RM 260 *	138
Paradise Suite	RM 300 *	140
Family Suite (2-Bdrm)	RM 500 *	20

* All rates are inclusive of 10% service charge and 5% government tax

Food & Beverage Outlets
Waves Restaurant - Located on Lower Lobby. For elegant dining in comfort. Western and Asian a la carte cuisine. Guests can either dine indoors or alfresco on the terrace overlooking the swimming pool.
Pantai Garden - Open atrium restaurant dining offering casual, breezy setting for buffet and theme dinners.
Pool Bar - Laze with delightful tropical drinks and snacks by the pool. An excellent area to rest and watch the sunset.
(In-room dining - Room Service meals for breakfast, lunch, dinner and supper)

Salsa Lounge - Just the setting to unwind and leave the day's toils behind. Relax in our comfy chairs and enjoy the pleasant atmosphere or waltz over to the Foosball and Pool corner for an enjoyable game.

Amenities, Facilities and Services
Conference & banquet halls facilities, Babysitting services, Babycots, Laundry and Dry Cleaning services including Self-Service Laundry Room, Mail and postage, Courier services, Luggage storage, Internet cafe, 24-hour security, Medical services (Doctors on call), Parking facilities, Tour desk and limousine services, Foreign exchange, Secretarial services, City Shuttle services **Room Amenities, Facilities & Services** - 300 elegant and fully furnished sea-facing suites with private balcony, Studio to one bedroom and two bedroom suites, Satellite television includes CNN, HBO, Discovery Channel, Starsports and Cartoon Network, IDD (International direct dialing telephones), Kitchenette, Coffee and tea making facilities, Hairdryer, Air-conditioning with individual control **Recreation** - Swimming pool, Tennis court, Squash court, Dart board, Volleyball court (beachfront), Seasports facilities, Gymnasium, Leisure activities for both adults and children, Reflexology

Arcade
Souvenir shop / Drug store, Hair and beauty salon

Credit Cards Accepted
American Express, Diners Club, JCB, MasterCard, Visa

Just call us for our
"Seasonal Guest Special "

Paradise Tanjung Bungah - Penang

505 Jalan Tanjung Bungah, 11200 Penang, Malaysia
Telephone : (60-4) 890 8808
Facsimile : (60-4) 890 8333
Email : beach@po.jaring.my
Web page : http://www.paradisehotel.com

Handbook Notes
Only 5 minutes from the city centre and 45 minutes from Penang International Airport.

Accommodation	Standard	Number
Superior Hillview	RM 195 *	95
Deluxe Seaview	RM 215 *	80
Superior Hillview Suite	RM 260 *	9
Delux Seaview Suite	RM 300 *	15
Presidential Seaview Suite	RM 500 *	1

Extra Bed - RM 40 *
* All rates are inclusive of 10% service and 5% government tax.

Food & Beverage Outlets
Shores Restaurant - Serves breakfast and lunch only.

Amenities, Facilities and Services
Swimming pool with children's pool, Fitness & health centre, Video games room, Beach & water sports, City shuttle services, Golf tee-off services can be made, Secretarial Services, Ample parking, Remote - controlled colour television, Laundry services, Refrigerator, Complimentary tea & coffee making facilities.

Shopping Arcade
Drugstore - Located at ground level - Lobby

Credit Cards Accepted
American Express, Diners Club, JCB MasterCard, Visa

Conference & Banqueting (MICE) Facilities
Banquet facilities available on request. Choice of 5 function halls of vrious sizes accommodating from 12 - 500 persons with full range of support facilities.

KDU Penang

32 Jalan Anson, 10400 Penang, Malaysia
Telephone : (60-4) 228 0053
Facsimile : (60-4) 228 0054
E-mail : best@kdupg.edu.my
Website : http://www.kdupg.edu.my

Handbook Notes
Whether it is pre-university, undergraduate, postgraduate courses, you can begin your pursuit of a recognized degree or qualification at KDU Penang. Since its inception in 1991, KDU Penang has sustained a reputation for quality in education offering selected prestigious degress from Australian, British and American universities at an affordable price.

Fast Facts
Number of students: 2,500
% of international students: 15
Countries: Thailand; Hong Kong; Indonesia; Nigeria; Siberia; Korea; Japan; Taiwan; China; Sweden; Bangladesh; Pakistan; Myanmar.
Number of full-time teaching staff: 60

10+1 Reasons to Choose KDU Penang
* 3+0 Programmes - Foreign degrees completed at a reduced cost
* Flexible course structure
* Interactive web-based learning
* Qualified academic staff
* Biggest Engineering School in the Northern Region
* One of the biggest Computing and Information Systems school in Malaysia
* 4-star hotel training facilities
* 1st college to acquire Internet access via leased line
* 1st college with an iMac Language Lab - complete with 20+ iMac computers
* 1st college with a Notebook Computer Lab - equipped with 40 Gateway Pentium II Notebooks; costing more than RM400,000
* Links with more than 300 universities in Australia, New Zealand, Switzerland, UK and US

Our Courses

	Duration
American University Studies	
Advanced Associate of Arts Diploma (AAAD)	24 mths
Advanced Associate of Science Diploma (AASD)	24 mths
KDU-Northwood University Program (BBA)	16 mths
B.Sc. in Business Admin. (Touro Univ. International)	via Internet
Business	
Foundation for Univ. Studies in Business	8 mths
KDU Certificate in Business Administration	3 1/2 - 8 mths
ABE/SBP (UK) Dip./Adv. Dip. in Business Admin.	6 - 12 mths
Murdoch University Twinning Programme	2 yrs
B. Commerce (Murdoch Univ.)	3 yrs
Computing & Information Systems	
Higher Diploma in Computer Studies	20 mths
Graduate Diploma in Information Technology	1 yr
B.Sc.(Hons) in Computer & Info. Science (ULH)	3 yrs
Engineering	
Dip. in Telecomm.,Electronic & Comp. Engineering	2 yrs
B.Eng.(Hons) in Electronic & Electrical Engineering	2 yrs
B.Eng.(Hons)/G.Dip. in Electronics & Comm. Systems	3 yrs
Arts and Science	
GCE A-Level Science/Humanities	10 - 13 mths
Intensive English	3 1/2 mths
IELTS 3 mths	
Hotel & Tourism Management	
KDU-IMI Swiss Cert. in Culinary Skills & Restaurant Services 1yr 4mths	
KDU-IMI Swiss Cert. in Professional Chef Training	1 yr 4 mths
KDU-IMI Diploma in Hotel & Catering Management	2 yrs 4 mths
KDU-IMI Diploma in Professional Chef Training	2 yrs

Our Semester Intakes
January, April, August

Our Fee Range
Between RM 4,000 to RM 12,000 per annum (varies according to the different programmes)

Our Facilities
Cyber Career Corner (Reception, Ground Floor) - To help you find the most appropriate careers through our online Career Assessment Test, as well as receiving on-line counselling through the college's Counselling Expert System. Open Hours: 9am-8pm (Weekdays) 9am - 4pm (Sat)
KDU-Gateway Corridor (Foyer, Ground Floor) - Equipped with 10 Gateway PC's for the use of high school students in developing an active e-learning culture.
Computer Labs (2nd Floor) - Workshop Lab, Internet Lab, Classroom Lab, Multimedia Lab. Open Hours: 9am - 9pm(Weekdays) 9am - 4pm (Weekends)
KDU-Gateway Notebook Computer Lab - For students only
Engineering & Science Labs (2nd Floor) - Open daily upon request
Multi-purpose hall
4-star Hotel & Tourism Training facilities ~ Bon Appetit Restaurant (Ground Floor) - A training restaurant for the Hotel & Tourism management students; production, preparation, pastry & cold kitchen facilities. Open Hours: noon -2pm (Tues for Set-Lunch), noon - 2pm (Thurs for ala Carte) ~ Mock-up Hotel Suite (1st Floor) - For students use only
Library (4th Floor) - Open Hours: 9am - 7pm (Mon- Tues), 9am - 9pm (Wed), 9am -7pm (Thurs), 9am - 5pm (Sat), Closed: Sundays & public holidays (subject to changes)
Resource Centre (1st Floor) - Open: 9am - 5.30pm (Weekdays), 9am - 1pm (alternate Sat)
Basketball and Volleyball Court
KDU Convenient Store(Ground Floor)

Our Societies
AUTP Society; ABE Society; Badminton; Bowling Club; College Christian Fellowship; Computer Club; Choir Club; Catholic Youth Group; Dance, Music & Drama; Editorial Board; Engineering Club; Ice Skating Club; Indian Cultural Society; International Club; IRAD; Leo Club; Murdoch Club; Punjabi Society; Rover Crew; Student Council; Taekwondo Club.

Support Services
Department of Student Affairs (DSA); Accommodation; Scholarships; University placements; Personal counselling; International Students Office; Free Internet & E-mail for all students.

Financial Aid
KDU Entrance Scholarships; KDU Merit Scholarships; KDU Sports Award; Tun Omar Yoke Lin Ong Scholarships; MAPCO Scholarships; The Star Education Fund.

Credit Cards Accepted
Master Card, Visa

LohGuanLye SPECIALISTS CENTRE

19 Jalan Logan 10400 Penang, Malaysia
Telephone : (60-4) 228 8501
Facsimile : (60-4) 229 0287

Handbook Notes
Situated in the heart of town and about 20 minutes away from the airport and Ferringhi beach. Loh Guan Lye Specialists Centre is a 250-bed private hospital. Established in 1975, the Centre is equipped for the practice of major disciplines of medicine.

Out-patient Specialists' Consultant Fees
During Office Hours
9:00 am - 5.00 pm (Weekdays)
9:00 am - 1.00 pm (Saturday)

* First Consultation	RM 45 - 90
* Follow up	RM 35 - 70

After Office Hours (Sundays & Public Holidays)

* First Consultation	RM 90.00
* Follow up	RM 70.00

Other Charges

Delivery Room	RM 80.00
Nursery (per Day)	RM 30.00
Incubator (per Day)	RM 50.00

Specialist Services
* Anaesthesiology
* Cardiology
* Child Development & Assessment
* Dental & Oral Surgery
* Endoscopic Surgery
* Ear, Nose, Throat, Head & Neck Surgery
* Epidural Anaesthesia
* Eye Surgery (including small incision Cataract Surgery)
* Gastroenterology, Hepatology & Therapeutic Endoscopy
* General Surgery, Chest Surgery & Urology (including Transurethral & Endourology)
* Internal Medicine & Medical Check-up
* Laparoscopic Surgery
* Laser Surgery
* Nephrology
* Neurology
* Neuro Surgery
* Obstetrics & Gynaecology

Specialist Services (cont'd)
* Oncology
* Orthopaedics Surgery, Sports Medicine & Bone Transport
* Paediatric Audiology & Neonatalogy
* Plastic, Reconstructive & Cosmetic Surgery (Hand & Micro Surgery)
* Psychology (Education & Counselling)
* Speech & Language Pathology/Therapy

Medical Services, Amenities & Facilities
Out-Patient (24 hours), Ambulance Service, Ambulatory

Medical Serivces, Amenities & Facilities (cont'd)
ECG, Five Delivery Suites, Five well equipped Major Operating Theatres, Intensive & Critical Care Units, Neonatal Intensive Care Unit, Nursery, Wards - Medical, Surgical, Paediatric, Obstetrics & Gynaecology and Deluxe Ward (an exclusive ward comprising of only suites and single rooms) Dialysis unit, Endoscopy, ERCP, Day Surgery, Dietetic Counselling, Physiotherapy, Occupational Therapy, Sports Injury, Rehabilitation & Gym, Diagnostic Imaging Services - Magnetic Resonance Imaging (MRI), CT Scan, Fluoroscopy, General X-Ray, Ultrasound & Mammography, OPG, Bone Densitometer, Laboratory, Pharmacy, Medical Officer services.

Other Hospital Amenities, Facilities & Services
Reception, Cafeteria, Private Lodgers' Rooms

Arcade
Koperasi Specialists Berhad D'Shoppe - Where you can get all your necessities

Visiting Hours
12.00 pm - 2.00 pm
5.00 pm - 10.00 pm

Hospital Deposits & Charges

Room	Rate per Day	Deposit Required	Nursing Care	Set Meals	Lodger
Adult/Paediatric Ward					
Single Room	RM 230.00	RM 3,000.00	RM 35.00	RM 10.00	RM 20.00
Double-Bedded	RM 110.00	RM 2,500.00	RM 25.00	RM 10.00	RM 20.00
General Ward	RM 65.00	RM 1,500.00	RM 20.00	RM 10.00	N/A
Intensive Care Unit	RM 220.00	RM 10,000.00	RM 50.00	N/A	N/A
Deluxe Ward					
Deluxe Suite	RM 600.00	RM 8,000.00	RM 65.00	Ala-carte	RM 60.00
Superior Suite	RM 500.00	RM 8,000.00	RM 65.00	Ala-carte	RM 60.00
Single Deluxe	RM 320.00	RM 5,000.00	RM 45.00	Ala-carte	RM 40.00
Single Superior	RM 270.00	RM 5,000.00	RM 45.00	Ala-carte	RM 40.00

Island Hospital

308 Macalister Road 10350, Penang, Malaysia
Telephone : (60-4) 228 8222
Facsimile : (60-4) 226 7989
Emergency: (60-4) 226 8527
E-Mail : info@islandhospital.com

Handbook Notes
Island Hospital is a 240 bed private medical centre situated in the heart of Georgetown, Penang. Its modern design is a landmark in hospital architecture, with its emphasis on uncluttered open spaces and friendly integrated units whose concept is in itself therapeutic for patient. It offers a wide range of medical, surgical and emergency services 24 hours a day.

Outpatient Specialists' Consultant Fees
During Office Hours
8:30 a.m. - 5:00 p.m. (Weekdays)
8:30 a.m. - 1:00 p.m. (Saturday)

* First Consultation	RM 50.00
* Follow Up	RM 35.00
* Special Consultation	RM 65.00 - RM 100.00

After Office Hours (Sundays & Public Holidays)

* First Consultation	RM 100.00
* Follow Up	RM 70.00
* Special Consultation	RM 100.00 - RM 200.00

Outpatient Specialists' Consultant Fees (cont'd)
Other Charges

Delivery Room	RM 150.00 / RM 200.00
Bassinette (per Day)	RM 30.00
Incubator (per Day)	RM 40.00

Medical Service Amenities & Facilities
Emergency Services (24 hours), Dietetic Counselling, Anaesthesiology & Intensive Care, Cardiology, Cardiothoracic Surgery, Ear, Nose and Throat Surgery, General Surgery, Gastroenterology/Hepatology, Hand Surgery and Microsurgery, Internal Medicine, Laparoscopic Surgery, Nephrology/Haemodialysis, Neurology, Obstetrics and Gynaecology, Ophthalmic Surgery, Orthopaedics and Trauma Surgery, Paediatric Medicine & Neonatology, Paediatric Surgery, Radiology and MRI, Urology/Lithotripsy, HeartScan, Physiotherapy, Rehabilitation, Clinical Laboratory, IVF Laboratory & Fertility Centre, Refractive Eye Surgery.

Other Hospital Amenities, Facilities & Services
Reception, Cafeteria, Garden, Gift Shop, Bakery Shop.

Visiting Hours
12:00 p.m. - 2:00 p.m.
5:00 p.m. - 8:00 p.m.

Hospital Deposits & Charges

Room	Rate per Day	Deposit	Nursing Care	Lodger	Food(Adult)	Food(Child)
Super Deluxe	RM 600.00	RM 8,000.00	RM 50.00	RM 50.00	RM 75.00	RM 50.00
Single Deluxe	RM 350.00	RM 5,000.00	RM 50.00	RM 50.00	RM 75.00	RM 50.00
Single Private	RM 250.00	RM 3,000.00	RM 30.00	RM 30.00	RM 50.00	RM 30.00
Two-Bedded	RM 120.00	RM 2,000.00	RM 20.00	RM 20.00	RM 25.00	RM 15.00
General Ward	RM 70.00	RM 1,500.00	RM 20.00	N/A	RM 25.00	RM 15.00
Intensive/ Coronary Care Unit	RM 220.00	RM 6,000.00	RM 30.00	N/A	RM 20.00	RM 15.00

* No charge for (1) lodger for paediatric patients
* All room rates/lodger/meals are subject to 5% GST
* Deposit for surgical cases vary. Please discuss this with surgeon.
* Day Ward - Bed and Nursing RM70.00, Food RM 10.00

All published rates are subject to change without notice

Strand Specialist Hospital

1 Persiaran Cempaka, Bandar Amanjaya
08000 Sungai Petani, Kedah
Telephone : (60-4) 442 8888
Facsimile : (60-4) 442 8889
E-mail : strand99@tm.net.my
Website : www.strandhospital.com.my

Handbook Notes
Located along the North-South Highway, by the Sungai
Petani North Toll outlet in Kedah, the Strand Specialist
Hospital is set in 3 acres of landscaped surroundings.
This fully air-conditioned and equipped establishment
provides quality specialist healthcare for the Northern region
of Peninsular Malaysia. The Strand's Geriatic &
Rehabilitation Centre facilities allow for 24-hour and
individualised nursing care with recreational and
occupational activities.

Out-patient Specialists' Consultant Fees
During Office Hours
9:00am - 5:00pm (Weekdays)
9:00am - 1:00pm (Saturday)

* First Consultation	RM	35.00
* Follow up	RM	25.00

After Office Hours (Sundays & Public Holidays)

* First Consultation	RM	70.00
* Follow up	RM	50.00
* Medical Officer	RM	30.00

From 12.00 Midnight to 6.00am

* First Consultation	RM	80.00
* Follow up	RM	60.00
* Medical Officer	RM	40.00

Other Charges

Nursery (per Day)	RM	20.00
Day Case (Deposit)	RM	1,500.00
Colonoscopy(Deposit)	RM	800.00
Endoscopy(Deposit)	RM	500.00

Medical Services & Consultant Specialists

Anaesthesiology	Ear, Nose & Throat Surgery
General Medicine	General Surgery
Obstetrics & Gynaecology	Opthalmology
Orthopaedics	Paediatrics & Neonatology
Radiology	

Medical Service Amenities & Facilities
Specialists Out Patient Clinics, Pharmacy, Clinical
Laboratory, Operating Theatre Suites, Day Use Wards,
Intensive Care Unit, Labour Room & Nursery, Special
Care Baby Unit, Haemodialysis Centre, Diagnostic Imaging
Services, Helical CT Scan, Echo-Cardiography, ECG &
Stress Test, Geriatic Care Unit, 24-hour Accident &
Emergency Unit, Day Surgery, Physiotherapy, 24-hour
Ambulance Service

Visiting Hours
12:00pm - 2:00pm
5:00pm - 8:00pm

Other Hospital Amenities & Charges

Room	Rate per Day	Deposit Required	Nursing Care	Set Meals
VIP	RM 280.00	RM 3,000.00	RM60.00	RM 30.00
Single	RM 160.00	RM 2,500.00	RM 20.00	RM 15.00
2 bedded	RM 75.00	RM 2,000.00	RM 20.00	RM 12.00
4 bedded	RM 50.00	RM 1,500.00	RM 20.00	N/A
ICU	RM 180.00	RM 3,000.00	RM 30.00	N/A

Geriatic & Rehabilitation Centre Charges and Deposits

Room	Rate per Day	per Week	per Fortnight	per Month
Category A	Single	RM 170.00	RM 1,070.00	RM 2,.020.00	RM 3,690.00
Bedridden, requiring frequent turning	2 Bedded	RM 90.00	RM 570.00	RM 1,070.00	RM 1,950.00
and all round nursing care.	4 Bedded	RM 70.00	RM 440.00	RM 840.00	RM 1,520.00
Catogory B	Single	RM 150.00	RM 940.00	RM 1,790.00	RM 3,260.00
Requiring assistance with dressing	2 Bedded	RM 80.00	RM 500.00	RM 950.00	RM 1,730.00
and feeding and mobilising	4 Bedded	RM 65.00	RM 410.00	RM 655.00	RM 1,420.00
Category C	Single	RM 135.00	RM 850.00	RM 1,610.00	RM 2,930.00
Requiring supervision only with	2 Bedded	RM 70.00	RM 440.00	RM 830.00	RM 1,520.00
dressing and feeding	4 Bedded	RM 55.00	RM 350.00	RM 655.00	RM 1,190.00
Category D	Single	RM 130.00	RM 820.00	RM 1,540.00	RM 2,820.00
Fully independent	2 Bedded	RM 65.00	RM 410.00	RM 770.00	RM 1,420.00
	4 Bedded	RM 50.00	RM 320.00	RM 590.00	RM 1,080.00

Category E
Daily Respite Care between 08:00 & 17:00
each day charged at 4 bed rate for relevant
category, paid weekly in advance

Rate per Day
Category A - RM 70.00
Category B - RM 65.00
Category C - RM 55.00
Category D - RM 50.00

Deposit
For all categories

Single   - RM 5,000.00
2 Bedded   - RM 4,000.00
4 Bedded   - RM 2,500.00

The Art Gallery

368-4-8 Burma Road
Bellisa Row, Pulau Tikus
Penang 10350, Malaysia
Telephone: (60-4) 229 8219
Facsimile : (60-4) 228 6714

Showroom at Level 2, Unit 7
Telephone: (60-4) 2276 986
Open daily except Mondays - 11am to 4pm

Main Exhibition Hall at Level 4, Unit 8
Telephone: (60-4) 2298 219
Open daily except Mondays - 11am to 6pm

Handbook Notes
Located at Bellisa Row along Jalan Burmah in Pulau Tikus, The Art Gallery, Penang, will be 12 years old in September 2001. From January 1999, visitors can now view two exhibitions simultaneously when they visit The Art Gallery at Bellisa Row. In addition to the regular exhibitions at the Main Exhibition Hall at Level 4, unit 8, there is now at Level 2, unit 7, an additional exhibition which changes every two months.

THE ART GALLERY, started in 1989 is located at level 4, unit 8 of the 5 storey Bellisa Row shopping complex in the prestigious suburb of Pulau Tikus. An additional showroom is at level 2, unit 7 of the same building.

It stocks paintings of Malaysian and International artists with particular focus on pioneer artists of Malaysia, Singapore and Indonesia. It also provides for prints including limited edition prints by Picasso and Chagall. The Gallery's Chinese brush (ink) paintings are sourced directly from the artists in China, eg. Tan Changrong, Li Baoyi, Du Ziling etc.

Apart from its representation of the works of over 30 artists, the Art Gallery also publishes over 20 books on Malaysian art, including the following:

1	Penang Artists 1920 - 1990 (1990)
2	Tan Choon Ghee Retrospective (1992)
3	Tan Peng Hooi - Oil Paintings (1993)
4	Pioneers of Malaysian Art (1994)
5	Lee Joo For Retrospective (1995)
6	Lee Long Looi Retrospective (1997)
7	Toya Retrospective (1997)
8	Social Responsibility in Art Criticism (1998)
9	Compendium of 30 Malaysian Artists (1999)
10	Malaysian Artists Vol. 1 & Vol. 2 (2001)

The Art Gallery is especially strong in paintings by the following Malaysian artists:-

Chai Chuan Jin	(born 1943)
Cheah Ewe Hoon, Miss	(born 1950)
Dr. Chew Teng Beng	(born 1938)
Chia Yu Chian	(1936 - 1991)
Chong Hon Fatt	(born 1941)
Choo Beng Teong	(born 1966)
Datuk Chuah Thean Teng	(born 1914)
Foo Hong Tat	(born 1940)
Fung Yow Chork	(born 1918)
Heng Eow Lin	(born 1946)
Ho Hee Khim	(born1948)
Ho Khay Beng	(1934 - 1986)

Khaw Sia	(1913 - 1984)
Malaysian Artists (cont'd)	
Khoo Sui Ho	(born 1939)
Khor Ean Ghee	(born 1934)
Kuo Ju Ping	(1908 - 1962)
Lee Cheng Yong	(1913 - 1974)
Lee Joo For	(born 1929)
Lee Long Looi	(born 1943)
Datuk Mohd Hoessein Enas	(1924 - 1995)
Eric Quah	(born 1946)
Tan Choon Ghee	(born 1930)
Tan Peng Hooi	(born 1944)
Datuk Tay Hooi Keat	(1910 - 1989)
Teh Siew Joo	(born 1930)
Toya (Lim Khoon Hock)	(born 1943)
Yong Mun Sen	(1896 - 1962)
Yeo Hoe Koon	(born 1935)
Dr Zakaria Ali	(born 1946)
Zulkifli Yusoff	(born 1961)

For more information, please contact
Miss Tan Ee Lene
Telephone: (60-4) 229 8219
Facsimile: (60-4) 228 6714

Please Note:
The Art Gallery will cease operations
on 31st December 2001.

ClayCraft /Slice Furniture

24, Moulmein Road, Pulau Tikus, 10350 Penang,
Malaysia.
Telephone : (604) 227 3622
Facsimile : (604) 227 3611

Lot 245 & 247, Rasa Sayang Resort Shopping
Arcade, Batu Feringgi, 11100 Penang, Malaysia.
Telephone : (604) 881 2228

20 Jalan 25/70A, Desa Sri Hartamas
50480 Kuala Lumpur, Malaysia.
Telephone : (603) 430 1396
Facsimile : (603) 430 1408

Lot 304, Level 3, Suria KLCC
50088 Kuala Lumpur, Malaysia.
Telephone / Facsimile : (603) 382 0183

Handbook Notes

Claycraft is a showcase for contemporary Malaysian
arts and crafts, housing the largest collection of gifts
and household accessories under one roof. Besides the
local and Asean hand-made ceramics, Slice Furniture
and Lighting and Minus Zero Boutique and Gallery
complete an entire lifestyle philosophy.

Tableware Art
with a function.
Includes a range
of in-house
designed and
manufactured
special items:
chopstick bowls,
sculptural teapots,
oblong vessels,
bum bowls, wire-
coil vases and
ashtrays, kama-
sutra oil lamps, 3-
legged dishes and much more.

Batik Textiles Hand-painted 100% cotton
experimenting with the age-old Malaysian tradition of
wax resist. Designs are inspired by tropical seas,
monsoons and rainforest textures.

Fused Glass Bowls, plates, platters and art pieces by
a local stained glass artist.

Water Jars A sculptural accent in the home and an
element of fengshui in the garden.

Boutique Tiles
Hand-finished
Celadon glaze or
custom-made
small produc-
tions.

***Gifts and
Household
Accessories***
Chopsticks, photo frames, breakfast trays, namecard
holders, display trays, trinket boxes, incense holders,
hemp bags, cd racks etc.

Furniture Using exotic regional materials such as
bamboo, rattan, palm wood, recycled hardwood,
juxtaposed with aluminium, steel, glass and perspex.

Lighting
From rattan
pendant shades
using traditional
materials to
starckly modern
aluminium
diffuse wall
lights.

Sunshine Square

Jalan Mahsuri, Bayan Baru, 11950 Penang, Malaysia
Telephone   : (60-4) 641 1111
Facsimile   : (60-4) 642 8888
E-mail   : suiwah@po.jaring.my
Home Page: http://www.jaring.my/suiwah

Handbook Notes
Located in Penang's fast-growing Bayan Baru township. Just 15 minutes from George Town and 5 minutes from the island's International Airport. Core shopping complex of Bayan Baru's commercial centre, offering foods, recreation and bargains!

Basement
Bank - Bank Simpanan Nasional and Southern Bank ATM serivces
Supermarket - Part of the Lai Lai chain of supermarket outlets with a comprehensive range of local and imported products
Ready-to-Eat Snack Walk - Where a changing variety of western and asian bite-foods like mini corn pancakes and herbal eggs can be sampled when you feel just a bit hungry
Bakery - Fresh breads, pastries, savouries and cakes galore!
Pharmacy - Provides proprietary and prescription medication including specialised dental and health care products
Chinese Medicine Hall - Herbs to heal, strengthen & revitalise
Liquor & Wines - Comprehensive range of Chinese and western wines and spirits including VSOPs, XOs, whiskies, tequilas, rums, rice wines and telephone cards(!)
Florist - Fresh *Flowers-To-Go*!
Locksmith & Stickers - Offers you key duplicating service as well as a variety of padlocks, key chains, fancy stickers and helmets for sale

Ground Floor (Road Level)
Anggrik Biru - Restaurant serving malay halal food
McDonald's - Yes. Ronald McD is here at Sunshine, too!
Nova (Bakery & Cafe) - A delicatessan offering sandwiches and pastries, cakes & savouries

Level 1
Electrical Department - Shop and view all major names in colour TVs, CD and VCD players, sound systems, and household electrical aplliances & accessories
Leading Excellent (M) Sdn. Bhd. - Provides easy payment schemes for electrical products
Do-It-Yourself (D-I-Y) Department - For gardening and home repair tools and accessories including plant care products
A & W - The root beer fast food outlet
Jia-Yen Noodles Cafe - Noodle dishes with choice of toppings
Naka Colour - Photo processing and camera film sales outlet
Sunshine Card Member Service Counter
Maybank Forex
Lead System - 'BESTA' talking dictionary
Pacific Style Holiday - Your convenient travel planner?
Royal Selangor - Malaysia's first name in pewterware
Sealite Optical - Fashion and prescription eyewear products
Time Galarie - Clocks, watches, digital and classic, all here!
Wywy Shop, Teleshop - Two home and hand phone outlets for variety and value-for-money!
Information & Consumer Service Counter - Gift vouchers, Telephone cards, Postage stamps, Newspapers, Newspaper ad placements, Pos Laju (Express Mail), Lost & Found, Gift wrapping services, Complaints, Information, Paging services
Sales Department - Special delivery & bulk purchase services, Credit facilities for bulk orders, Consignment products to cooperative stores, Incentives point-system for company employees, Cosmetic promotions at store premises

Level 1A
Sunshine Food Garden - Local delicacies

Level 2
Men's Wear - JEANS - Baleno, Bendix , Camel, GQ, JC Benny, Lee Cooper, Oxen, Texan EXECUTIVE WEAR - Crocodile, Dapper, Durban, Elba, GMV, John Master, Milano, Orlando, Snails FOOTWEAR - Asadi, Bata, Johnson, Larrie, Marelli, Mizuno, Pallas,Puma, Reebok SPORTSWEAR - Carpenter

Level 2 (cont'd)
Cheetah, Crocodile Sports, Forest, Mizuno, Nike, Schwarzenbach TEENAGE LIFESTYLE - B.U.M., Chargers, Diesel
Auano Menswear • *Men's Undergarment and Accessories* • *Men's Swimwear Department* • *Luggage Department* • *Sports/ Fishing Equipment and Hobbies*
Delifrance French Cafe - For pastries and deli sandwiches with your choice of filling. Hot and cold drinks

Level 2A
Hitwaves - Music heaven with jazz, rock, blues, pop, classics and all other music in CDs, cassettes, tape for your collection
WyWy Wonderspace - Video games

Level 3
Ladies' Department - Ladies' Wear • Costume Jewellery • Handbags • Shoes • Undergarment
Children & Baby Products - BABY CLOTHES - Anakku, Baby Kiko, Disney, Baby W.O.C., Freedom, Pride & Joy, Tollyjoy BABY CARE PRODUCTS - Johnson & Johnson, Pureen, Diapers CHILDREN'S CLOTHES - American Athletics, Biz Kid, Cheetah Junior, Colour Fun, Cute Maree, Poney, Kiki Lala, Kiko, W.O.C. Kids CHILDREN'S SHOES - Asadi, Grace, Kiki Lala, Sesame Street, Tom & Jerry
Cosmetics Department - Fragrance, Juju, Kose, Max Factor, Shiseido
Ladies' Jeanswear - American Athletics, Half, Hapy, Nature Project, Tuff, Voir Jeans
Riche Jewellery
Textiles Department
Malay Costume

Level 3A
Event Hall

Level 4
Household Department - Baby Carriages, Cotton Goods, DIY Furniture, Glassware, Home Furnishing, Plasticware
Crystal House - Crystalware for decoration and as gifts
Orient Jewellers - All that glitters that *is* gold
Public Watch - Watches & Clocks. Local & Imported
Spring Garden - Sewing accessories
Sunshine Book - Chinese & English Book Retail Outlet
Stationery & Gifts - Including novelties, music boxes, souvenirs to suit all tastes
Toys Department - A little heaven for the young

Level 5
Sun Garden Chinese Restaurant - Featuring Chinese cuisine
Top Bowl Bowling Centre - 32-Lane Bowling Centre with eating area serving snacks & beverages

BUSINESS HOURS:	LEVELS 1-4	BASEMENT SUPERMARKET
Mon-Fri	12noon - 10pm	12noon - 10:30pm
Sat., Sun. & Pub Holidays	10:00am - 10pm	10:00am - 10:30pm

Disc & Dat

125-G Desa Tanjung, Jalan Tanjung Tokong,
10470 Penang, Malaysia
Telephone : (60-4) 899 0864
Facsimile : (60-4) 899 0864

Handbook Notes
Located across the street of, and adjacent to Tanjung
Tokong's Island Plaza, Disc & Dat is arguably Penang's
most comprehensive music CD outlet. Served by young
and knowledgeable staff, the wide range of music
categories stocked at this outlet makes it a favoured
one-stop shop for local and expatriate music lovers.

The Disc & Dat Story

Dissatisfied with the selection available from purely
commercial music stores, Ivan, the often distracted
proprietor of Disc & Dat decided to satisfy his own passion
for music by opening a shop of his own in 1994. It was
not long before he was purchasing music CDs from
abroad to distinguish his store from all the others existing.
As he said, "Since I was already buying for my own
collection the music I enjoyed, I decided to go the whole
hog and buy quite a lot more, which a music outlet would
let me do." Before he knew it, Ivan had gained for himself
the following of loyal customers that he needed to expand
his store's musical selection as he wanted.

Today, the Disc & Dat is as much a club for music
lovers as it is a music store. His customers stroll in to
talk about everything from *Beethoven's Fifth* to the latest
from *Boyzone*. There is an almost bewildering selection

of New Age sound, Blues, Jazz, Heavy Metal, Classical,
good old fashioned Rock and Roll, as well as the oldies
from the 50's and 60's, including the latest groups that
are just making their mark in today's fast-moving world
of synthetic sound.

There is a growing number of retail outlets in Penang,
set up by individuals who have a passion for the products
they are dealing in. And the Disc & Dat is one such outlet
- providing a standard of service as well as a range of
products which can only make the life of a shopper that
much more a pleasure.

Business hours
Tuesdays - Saturdays : 11:00am to 8:30pm
Sundays : 2:00pm - 8.00pm
Mondays : Closed

Yahong Art Gallery Sdn. Bhd.

58-D, Batu Ferringhi Road, 11100 Penang, Malaysia
Telephone : (60-4) 881 1251
Facsimile : (60-4) 881 1093

Handbook Notes Located in the Batu Ferringgi beach
resort area, the Yahong Art Gallery is a short walk from
most of the major beach hotels there. The gallery is fully
air-conditioned to ensure a comfortable browse of its
extensive range of art and antiquities.

The **Yahong Art Gallery** is home to Malaysia's batik
artist, *Chuah Thean Teng*. Teng's original batik paintings,
coupled with the work of his three artist sons, are displayed
in the gallery's upper level. Teng's works are in private
collections and museums around the world.

Teng, whose notability as the father and master of
batik painting, has transformed the ancient craft of batik
into a fine art form. In addition, Teng's three sons are also
artists working in batik painting as well as several other
mediums.

Although Teng's paintings occupy a prominent position
in the gallery, Yahong also displays works of other notable
artists in watercolour, Chinese ink and oil. Yahong's engaging
display of vivid art works are meant for the casual buyer
as well as the serious collector.

Handicrafts - In the Gallery's lower levels, the visitor will
discover genuinely exotic gift items. An ancient Malaysian
medicine horn, a Sarawakian Chief's staff or exquisite
Chinese cloisonne, and extraordinary Chinese tile pictures.

Pewterware - Yahong offers a selection of the finest
Selangor Pewter, Malaysia's gift to the world. Choose
from coffee and tea sets, ale mugs and vases in both
traditional and modern variations. Or select a jewellery
case of collector's item to serve as a momento of your
stay in Malaysia.

Jewellery & Antiques - Yahong offers a wide selection of
fine Chinese jewellery made from jade, lapis lazuli and
other semiprecious stones. There are also distinctive
carvings from the very same semiprecious stones. The
gallery also has a fine selection of antique pieces for
collectors.

Gallery Hours are from 9.30am to 10.00pm

111

Penang International Sports Arena

Venue Manager : PenEvents Sdn. Bhd.
Jalan Tun Dr. Awang
11900 Penang
Telephone : (60-4) 645 1934
Facsimile : (60-4) 645 1953
E-mail : daniel@pisa.com.my

Handbook Notes

Located at the fastest growth township of Bayan Baru and close proximity to the Bukit Jambul commercial zone. Only 5 minutes away from the Penang International Airport and 20 minutes drive from the city center.

PISA comprises the Main Arena, the Aquatic Centre and a Multi-Storey Car Park Complex.

The Main Arena

A multi-purpose venue for
* Exhibitions
* Banquets
* Concerts
* Conventions
* Indoor Sports
* Corporate Events

The Aquatic Centre

An all weather swimming complex with:
* A competition pool with diving facilities
* A leisure pool

Amenities, Facilities and Services

Function rooms suitable for seminars, meetings and conferences with foldable partitions to cater for space requirements of different settings. *Sports Facilities* - Badminton courts, Vollyball courts, Sepak Takraw courts, Basketball courts and Table Tennis. *Other Services* - Event Management, Food & Beverage Arrangement, Event Security Services

Conference* & Banqueting** (MICE) Facilities

Venue	Area (m2)	Theatre	Classroom	Banquet	Buffet	Cocktail	Exhibitions
Level 2							
Main Arena	3,000	3,000	N/A	3,000	2,000	N/A	*
Function Room 1A	76.15	60	25	40	30	30	N/A
Function Room 1B	87.95	90	40	60	50	50	N/A
Function Room 1C	87.95	90	40	60	50	50	N/A
Function Room 1D	76.15	60	25	40	30	30	N/A
Function Room 1E	48.50	30	15	N/A	N/A	N/A	N/A
Function Room 1F	48.50	30	15	N/A	N/A	N/A	N/A
Level 3							
Concourse	3,415	N/A	N/A	4,000	4,000	N/A	*

Contact Directory

Category & Name of Contact	Contact Number	See Page
Accommodation		
- Beach Hotels & Resorts		
Bayview Beach Resort	(60-4) 881 2123	-
Casuarina Beach Resort	(60-4) 881 1711	102
Copthorne Orchid	(60-4) 890 3333	102
Crown Prince Hotel	(60-4) 890 4111	-
Ferringhi Beach Hotel	(60-4) 890 5999	-
Holiday Inn Resort	(60-4) 881 1601	-
Mutiara Beach Resort, Penang	(60-4) 885 2828	97
Paradise Sandy Bay Hotel	(60-4) 899 9999	103
Paradise Tanjung Bungah	(60-4) 890 8808	103
Parkroyal Beach Resort, Penang	(60-4) 881 1133	-
Shangri-La's Golden Sands Beach Resort	(60-4) 881 1911	99
Shangri-La's Rasa Sayang Beach Resort	(60-4) 881 1811	99
- Town & City Hotels		
Agora Hotel, Penang	(60-4) 226 6060	-
Appollo Hotel	(60-4) 331 1355	-
Berjaya Georgetown Hotel Penang	(60-4) 227 7111	-
Cabana Hotel	(60-4) 333 4366	-
Cathay Hotel	(60-4) 262 6271	-
Cititel Penang	(60-4) 370 1188	93
City Bayview Hotel, The	(60-4) 263 3161	94
Evergreen Laurel Hotel Penang	(60-4) 226 9988	96
Fortuna, Hotel	(60-4) 226 8282	-
Garden Inn Hotel	(60-4) 226 3655	-
Golden City, Hotel	(60-4) 227 9910	-
Grand Cotinental Hotel	(60-4) 263 6688	-
Hong Kong Hotel	(60-4) 890 8516	-
Hong Ping, Hotel	(60-4) 262 5243	-
International Hotel	(60-4) 226 2024	-
Malaysia, Hotel	(60-4) 263 3311	-
Merchant Inn Hotel, The	(60-4) 263 2828	-
Midtowne Hotel	(60-4) 226 9999	-
Mingood, Hotel	(60-4) 229 9922	-
New China Hotel	(60-4) 263 1601	-
Oriental, Hotel	(60-4) 263 4211	-
Peking Hotel	(60-4) 263 6191	-
Shangri-La Hotel	(60-4) 262 2622	98
Sheraton Hotel	(60-4) 226 7888	-
Sunway Hotel Penang	(60-4) 229 9988	101
Sunway Hotel Seberang Jaya	(60-4) 370 7788	-
Swiss Hotel	(60-4) 262 0306	-
Town House Hotel	(60-4) 263 8621	-
Waldorf Hotel	(60-4) 262 6141	-
White House Hotel	(60-4) 263 2385	-
- Island Hotels		
Hotel Equatorial	(60-4) 643 8111	95
- Service Apartments		
Mar Vista Resort	(60-4) 890 3388	-
Dining		
- Chinese		
Canton Palace	(60-4) 226 9988	96
Fu Ling Men Chinese Restaurant	(60-4) 370 1188	93
Golden Lotus	(60-4) 263 3161	94
Golden Phoenix	(60-4) 643 8111	95
House of Four Seasons Chinese Restaurant	(60-4) 885 2828	97
Hua Ting Chinese Restaurant	(60-4) 890 3333	102
Shang Court	(60-4) 881 1811	99
Shang Palace	(60-4) 262 2622	98
- Continental		
Le Bistro	(60-4) 643 8111	95
Brasserie, The	(60-4) 262 2622	98
Ferringhi Grill	(60-4) 881 1811	99

Category & Name of Contact	Contact Number	See Page
Dining		
- Continental (cont'd)		
View, The	(60-4) 643 8111	95
- Italian		
Il Ritrovo	(60-4) 881 1711	102
La Farfalla Italian Restaurant	(60-4) 885 2828	97
Peppino	(60-4) 881 1911	99
- Japanese		
Kampachi	(60-4) 643 8111	95
Kirishima Japanese Restaurant	(60-4) 370 1188	93
Tsuru-No-Ya Japanese Restaurant	(60-4) 885 2828	97
Waka	(60-4) 881 1811	99
- Western & Asian		
Café Laurel	(60-4) 226 9988	96
Casuarina Garden Terrace	(60-4) 881 1711	102
Equatorial Coffee Garden	(60-4) 643 8111	95
Golden Sands Garden Cafe	(60-4) 881 1911	99
Kopi Tiam	(60-4) 263 3161	94
Kuda Laut	(60-4) 881 1911	99
Mutiara Garden Terrace Restaurant	(60-4) 885 2828	97
Nutmegs	(60-4) 229 9988	101
Pantai Garden	(60-4) 899 9999	103
Revolving Restaurant, The	(60-4) 263 3161	94
Rasa Sayang Coffee Garden	(60-4) 881 1811	99
Rasa Sayang Garden Terrace	(60-4) 881 1811	99
Rasa Sayang Pool Bar, The	(60-4) 881 1811	99
Shangri-La Coffee Garden	(60-4) 262 2622	98
Shores Restaurant	(60-4) 890 8808	103
"Sigi's by the Sea" Bistro Bar	(60-4) 881 1911	99
Sunset Lounge	(60-4) 881 1911	99
Tepi Laut	(60-4) 881 1811	99
Terrace Bay	(60-4) 890 3333	102
Tropics Cafe	(60-4) 229 9988	101
Waves Restaurant	(60-4) 899 9999	103
Entertainment		
- Bars, Pubs, Lounges		
1st Avenue	(60-4) 370 1188	93
24-hour Main Street Café	(60-4) 370 1188	93
Asmara Lounge	(60-4) 881 1711	102
Blue Moon	(60-4) 643 8111	95
Casuarina Pool Bar	(60-4) 881 1711	102
City Bayview Lobby Lounge	(60-4) 263 3161	94
Copthorne Lobby Lounge	(60-4) 890 3333	102
Desperado's	(60-4) 262 2622	98
Evergreen Lobby Lounge	(60-4) 226 9988	96
Palmetto Lounge	(60-4) 885 2828	97
Passe Temps	(60-4) 643 8111	95
Rasa Sayang Lobby Lounge	(60-4) 881 1811	99
Salsa Lounge	(60-4) 899 9999	103
Sandy Bay Pool Bar	(60-4) 899 9999	103
Puppetry Lounge	(60-4) 885 2828	97
Shangri-La Lobby Lounge	(60-4) 262 2622	98
Tepi Laut Bar	(60-4) 881 1811	99
- Discotheques & Night Clubs		
Carmen N.Y. Club	(60-4) 263 3161	94
Shock Egypt Discotheque	(60-4) 890 3333	102
- Karaoke Lounge		
Crystal KTV Karaoke Bar/Lounge	(60-4) 370 1188	93
Stars Karaoke	(60-4) 890 3333	102

Please turn over

113

Contact Directory

Category & Name of Contact	Contact Number	See Page
Products & Services		
- Air Cargo Services		
Air Express International (m) SB	(60-4) 643 4033	-
Bax (m) SB	(60-4) 644 1795	-
Emery Worldwide (m) SB	(60-4) 643 7360	-
Hecny Transportation (m) SB	(60-4) 643 0936	-
Kintetsu Integrated Air Service SB	(60-4) 643 0927	-
MSAS Cargo International (m) SB	(60-4) 643 0044	-
TNT Express Worldwide (m) SB	(60-4) 642 0942	-
United Forwarding & Clearing SB	(60-4) 262 7070	-
- Air Charter & Rental		
Channel Five (m) SB	(60-4) 262 2345	-
Medic-Link SB	(60-4) 226 5577	-
Pan Malaysian Air Transport SB	(60-4) 644 5520	-
- Airline Companies		
Cathay Pacific Airways Ltd	(60-4) 226 0411	-
Emirates	(60-4) 263 1100	-
Eva Air Corporation	(60-4) 643 8244	-
KLM Royal Dutch Airlines Ltd (Cargo)	(60-4) 643 5500	-
Korean Airlines (Cargo)	(60-4) 644 2099	-
Lufthansa German Airlines (Cargo)	(60-4) 643 8943	-
Malaysian Airline System Bhd	(60-4) 262 0011	-
Singapore Airlines Ltd	(60-4) 226 3201	-
South African Airways	(60-4) 229 3318	-
Thai Airways International Ltd	(60-4) 226 6000	-
United Airlines	(60-4) 263 6020	-
- Antiques		
Clay Craft	(60-4) 227 3622	109
Yahong Art Gallery SB	(60-4) 261 7572	111
- Art & Craft, Batek, Paintings & Souvenirs		
Art Gallery, The	(60-4) 229 8219	108
Clay Craft	(60-4) 227 3622	109
Hong Giap	(60-4) 261 5129	-
Yahong Art Gallery SB	(60-4) 261 7572	111
- Banks		
ABN AMRO Bank Bhd	(60-4) 262 2144	-
AlliedBank (m) Bhd	(60-4) 332 1178	-
Arab Malaysian Bank Bhd	(60-4) 262 6266	-
Ban Hin Lee Bank Bhd	(60-4) 227 7882	-
Bank Bumiputra Malaysia Bhd	(60-4) 261 3753	-
Bank Islam (m) Bhd	(60-4) 262 6266	-
Bank of Commerce (m) Bhd	(60-4) 390 1577	-
Bank Persatuan (m) Bhd	(60-4) 333 7424	-
Bank Simpanan National	(60-4) 226 3278	-
Bank Utama (m) Bhd	(60-4) 390 1567	-
BSN Commercial Bank (m) Bhd	(60-4) 399 1900	-
Chung Khiaw Bank (m) Bhd	(60-4) 262 7348	-
CitiBank NA	(60-4) 226 5111	-
DCB Bank Bhd	(60-4) 262 5606	-
EON Bank Bhd	(60-4) 229 7288	-
Hock Hua Bank Bhd	(60-4) 658 6000	-
Hock Hua Bank (sabah) Bhd	(60-4) 227 3190	-
Hong Leong Bank Bhd	(60-4) 261 5561	-
Hongkong Bank (m) Bhd	(60-4) 262 9441	-
Kwong Yik Bank Bhd	(60-4) 262 5441	-
MayBank	(60-4) 261 2461	-
Multi-Purpose Bank Bhd	(60-4) 642 5918	-
OCBC Bank (m) Bhd	(60-4) 262 5301	-
Oriental Bank Bhd	(60-4) 226 4177	-
Overseas Union Bank (m) Bhd	(60-4) 261 1511	-
The Pacific Bank Bhd	(60-4) 281 0391	-
Perwira Affin Bank Bhd	(60-4) 262 0198	-
Public Bank Bhd	(60-4) 261 3415	-

Category & Name of Contact	Contact Number	See Page
Products & Services (cont'd)		
- Banks (cont'd)		
Sime Bank Bhd	(60-4) 262 1144	-
Southern Bank Bhd	(60-4) 261 9517	-
Standard Chartered Bank (m) Bhd	(60-4) 262 3000	-
United Overseas Bank (m) Bhd	(60-4) 262 2386	-
Wah Tat Bank Bhd	(60-4) 227 8222	-
- Boats Charter & Rental		
Mustafa Puteh	(60-4) 881 1488	-
Penang Marina Club & Resort SB	(60-4) 641 5609	-
- Bookshops		
Arthur's Books	(60-4) 641 5724	-
Children's World SB	(60-4) 261 5517	-
Evangel Book Centre	(60-4) 227 6431	-
Hong Heng Keong	(60-4) 281 0340	-
MPH Bookstores SB	(60-4) 899 9121	-
Nanyang Book Co (pg) SB	(60-4) 261 5986	-
Popular Book Co (m) SB	(60-4) 263 0682	-
Salvation Book Centre (m) SB	(60-4) 226 7617	-
Times Bookshop PL	(60-4) 228 0061	-
United Happy Stores	(60-4) 261 1293	-
- Car AirConditioning		
Autocold Air-Conditioning Centre	(60-4) 229 8753	-
Beng Auto Aircond Service	(60-4) 656 5781	-
Chin Lee Car Air Cond & Accessories	(60-4) 262 7764	-
Motor Cold Air Conditioning Centre	(60-4) 281 4312	-
- Clubs & Associations		
Alliance Francaise de Penang	(60-4) 227 6008	-
American Women's Association of Penang	(60-4) 228 0158	-
Automobile Association of Malaysia (AAM)	(60-4) 227 6051	-
British Council	(60-4) 263 0330	-
Chinese Recreation Club	(60-4) 226 7369	-
Chinese Swimming Club	(60-4) 899 0813	-
Malaysian-German Society	(60-4) 229 6853	-
Penang Consumers Association	(60-4) 229 3511	-
Penang Club	(60-4) 227 7366	-
Penang Japanese Association	(60-4) 229 3257	-
Penang Motor Sports Club	(60-4) 226 2059	-
Penang Rifle Club	(60-4) 226 2484	-
Penang Sports Club	(60-4) 229 7834	-
Penang Swimming Club	(60-4) 890 5720	-
Penang Turf Club	(60-4) 229 3233	-
Penang Yacht Club	(60-4) 228 3000	-
YMCA (Young Men's Christian Association)	(60-4) 229 2349	-
YWCA (Young Women's Christian Assocn.)	(60-4) 828 1855	-
- Consulates & Consulates-General (Please note that most consular offices are open for visa applications only from 9am to 12noon)		
Bangladesh, Hon. Consulate-General of	(60-4) 261 6296	-
British Representative at Penang, Hon.	(60-4) 262 5333	-
Danish Consulate, Royal	(60-4) 262 4886	-
Finland, Hon. Consulate of	(60-4) 227 7325	-
France, Hon. Consulate-Gen. of	(60-4) 292 9707	-
Germany, Hon. Consulate of	(60-4) 641 5707	-
Hungary, Hon. Consulate of the Rep. of	(60-4) 644 9937	-
Indonesia, Consulate-General of	(60-4) 227 4686	-
Japan, Consulate-General of	(60-4) 226 8222	-
Netherlands Hon. Consul, Royal	(60-4) 261 6471	-
Norwegian Consulate, Royal	(60-4) 262 5333	-
Russian Federation, Hon. Consulate of the	(60-4) 262 2944	-
Sri Lanka, Hon. Con. of	(60-4) 261 3093	-
Sweden, Consulate of	(60-4) 262 5333	-
Thai Conuslate-General, Royal	(60-4) 226 8029	-

Contact Category & Name	Contact Number	See Page
Products & Services (cont'd)		
- Consulates & Consulates-General (cont'd)		
Turkey, Hon. Consulate-Gen.of the Rep. of	(60-4) 261 5933	-
- Courier Services		
Asia Pacific Courier (m) SB	(60-4) 229 8042	-
City-Link Express (m) SB	(60-4) 281 3333	-
DHL Worldwide Express SB	(60-4) 642 8300	-
Federal Express Service (m) SB	1-800 88 6363	-
Nationwide Express Services SB	(60-4) 262 3107	-
Overseas Courier Service (m) SB	(60-4) 227 5290	-
Parceline (m) SB	(60-4) 229 0255	-
TNT Express Worldwide (m) SB	(60-4) 642 0942	-
United Parcel Service (m) SB	(60-4) 643 3530	-
- Duty Free Shops		
Kong Beng Duty Free Shop	(60-4) 229 0000	-
Pacific Prestige ProductsJewellerys SB	(60-4) 228 1414	-
Sriwani Tax Free Emporium SB	(60-4) 890 7217	-
- Electrical Goods & Appliances		
Ban Hin Bee SB	(60-4) 228 9880	-
Electrolux Home Appliances SB	(60-4) 829 0696	-
Hagemeyer (m) SB	(60-4) 261 4427	-
Kah Sales & Services (pg) SB	(60-4) 227 1332	-
Kim TV Audio Centre	(60-4) 226 9170	-
Pensonic Sales & Services SB	(60-4) 507 0393	-
Pertama Electronics & Photo SB	(60-4) 262 1491	-
Sanyo Sales & Service SB	(60-4) 657 1677	-
Sony Sales & Service (m) SB	(60-4) 399 6400	-
Star Radio Service	(60-4) 643 5948	-
- Florists		
Aurora Florist	(60-4) 829 4079	-
Bamboo Green Florist	(60-4) 331 5172	-
Charis Florist & Gift Centre	(60-4) 644 7088	-
Chooi Flowers & Gifts	(60-4) 826 8628	-
D'Bamboo Green Floral Design Centre SB	(60-4) 656 6288	-
Everlasting Florist & Handcraft	(60-4) 399 6779	-
Federal Florists	(60-4) 229 5043	-
Floral Creation	(60-4) 228 3832	-
Floral Touch SB	(60-4) 229 3623	-
Floramay Florist	(60-4) 262 2012	-
Florist De May	(60-4) 656 2320	-
Florist Hoka	(60-4) 228 4063	-
Flower Language Florist	(60-4) 899 2216	-
Fragrance Florist	(60-4) 263 4190	-
Greenery Flowers Corner	(60-4) 332 1097	-
Image Flowers & Gifts	(60-4) 228 2528	-
Joy Flowers & Gifts	(60-4) 261 6001	-
Lip Sin Floral Enterprise	(60-4) 645 2282	-
Morningstar Floral & Gift Centre	(60-4) 659 8032	-
Nina Flowers & Gifts Enterprises	(60-4) 229 7385	-
Nyonya House of Creations	(60-4) 641 3231	-
O'Hara Florist	(60-4) 228 6977	-
Orchard Florist	(60-4) 226 9823	-
Sunflora Florist Centre	(60-4) 644 6001	-
Yada Florist	(60-4) 658 8743	-
Yan Florist	(60-4) 644 6021	-
Yeo Yeo Enterprise	(60-4) 226 3212	-
- Jewellers		
B P De Silva (m) SB	(60-4) 226 5881	-
B P Goldsmith (m) SB	(60-4) 263 5868	-
Berkat Jewellers SB	(60-4) 261 6611	-
City Jewellers	(60-4) 261 7162	-
De Silva (m) SB	(60-4) 261 3093	-
Habib Jewels SB	(60-4) 261 2815	-

Category & Name of Contact	Contact Number	See Page
Products & Services (cont'd)		
- Jewellers (cont'd)		
Kim How Jewellers	(60-4) 261 2282	-
Nam Loong & Co SB	(60-4) 261 3400	-
- Local Products		
Cap Jempol Tropiks (pg) SB	(60-4) 263 6861	-
Ghee Hiang Holdings SB	(60-4) 262 0635	-
Him Heang SB	(60-4) 228 6129	-
Lim Wah Thai Local Food Products SB	(60-4) 228 1063	-
Tean Ean Local Products (m) SB	(60-4) 229 8130	-
- Medical Specialist Centres		
Penang Adventist Hospital	(60-4) 226 1133	-
Gleneagles Medical Centre Penang	(60-4) 227 6111	-
Island Hospital	(60-4) 226 1133	106
LohGuanLye Specialists Centre	(60-4) 228 8501	105
Pantai Mutiara, Hospital	(60-4) 643 3888	-
Strand Hospital & Retirement Home	(60-4) 442 8888	107
- Merchant Banks		
Arab-Malaysian Merchant Bank Bhd	(60-4) 226 1818	-
Malaysian Internat'lMerchant Bankers Bhd	(60-4) 228 3021	-
- Shopping Complexes		
Axis Complex	(60-4) 226 1816	-
Bukit Jambul Complex	(60-4) 641 1188	-
Gama Supermarket & Departmental Store	(60-4) 226 2111	-
Island Plaza	(60-4) 890 8888	-
KOMTAR	(60-4) 263 7570	-
Lai Lai Burmah	(60-4) 227 2299	-
Megamal Pinang	(60-4) 397 6688	-
Midlands Park Centre	(60-4) 226 3768	-
Penang Plaza	(60-4) 226 8080	-
Sunshine Square	(60-4) 641 1111	110
Transportation		
- Bus Companies		
Express Nasional Bhd	(60-4) 331 5986	-
Hosni Express SB	(60-4) 261 7746	-
Park May Bhd	(60-4) 229 8504	-
- Car Rental		
Avis Rent A Car	(60-4) 881 1522	-
Bakar Rent A Car	(60-4) 228 1541	-
Budget Car Rental	(60-4) 643 6025	-
Hawk Rent A Car	(60-4) 642 2455	-
Hertz Rent A Car	(60-4) 263 5914	-
Kasina Rent-A-Car	(60-4) 644 1842	-
Magic Green Rent A Car	(60-4) 643 7603	-
Mayflower Car Rental	(60-4) 262 8196	-
National Car Rental	(60-4) 262 9404	-
New Bob Rent A Car	(60-4) 226 6111	-
Orix Car Rentals SB	(60-4) 261 8608	-
Pacific Rent-A-Car	(60-4) 643 8891	-
Raya Car Rental	(60-4) 643 8891	-
Saber Car Rental	(60-4) 899 9666	-
Sintat Rent A Car	(60-4) 643 0958	-
SMAS Rent A Car	(60-4) 645 2288	-
- Taxi Services		
Auto Spin	(60-4) 262 3229	-
CT Radio Taxi Service	(60-4) 229 9467	-
Georgetown Transport & Tourist Service	(60-4) 229 5788	-
Jade Auto	(60-4) 226 3015	-
Perstn Kebajikan Empunya² Pemandu Teksi	(60-4) 263 4681	-
Sykt. Kenderaan Bekerjasama-sama SP	(60-4) 333 4459	-

Travel Notes

Geography   Penang is one of the States of Malaysia, situated on the north western coast of the peninsula. Bounded to the north and east by the State of Kedah & to the south by the State of Perak, it consists of the island of Penang (Pulau Pinang) and a coastal strip on the mainland called Province Wellesley (Seberang Prai). The island covers an area of 285 sq km. Its shape resembles a swimming turtle, and it is approximately 24 km north to south and 14.5 km east to west. The island and mainland are separated by a channel 3km wide at the closest point and 13km at the farthest. They are linked by the 13.5km Penang Bridge, the third longest in the world, and a 24-hour ferry service.

Climate   The climate is generally warm throughout the year with temperatures ranging from 21°C to 32°C. Humidity is generally high all year round. April, May and October are usually the wetter months.

Population   Penang has 1.2 million people, more than half of whom live on the island. The population is multi-racial, young and almost equally distributed between male and female.

Language & Religion   Bahasa Malaysia is the official language, but English is widely used in business and in the tourism industry. Reflecting the multiracial population, many Asian languages and dialects are spoken including Hokkien, Cantonese, Mandarin and Tamil. Islam is the official religion in Malaysia. However, Buddhism, Christianity, Hinduism, Sikhism, Taoism and other religions are freely practiced - visitors can expect to be disorientated by the diversity of religious celebrations and the profusion of mosques, temples and churches, quite commonly, side by side.

Entry Formalities

Passports   All visitors are required to be in possession of valid passports, or, in lieu of it, other internationally-recognised travel documents such as Certificates of Identity and Emergency Certificates of Affidavits, for travel to Malaysia. Such a passport or travel document must have at least 6 months validity beyond the period of stay permitted in the country.

Visas   *Nationals of Switzerland, Netherlands, San Marino, Liechtenstein as well as Commonwealth citizens (excepting those from India, Bangladesh, Pakistan & Sri Lanka)* do not need a visa to enter Malaysia as bona fide visitors. *Citizens of the following countries do not need visas for stays not exceeding 3 months if they hold full national passports*: Albania, Algeria, Argentina, Austria, Bahrain, Belgium, Czech

Republic, Denmark, Egypt, Finland, Germany, Hungary, Iceland, Italy, Japan, Jordan, Kuwait, Lebanon, Luxembourg, Morocco, Norway, Oman, Qatar, Saudi Arabia, Slovakia, South Korea, Sweden, Tunisia, Turkey, United Arab Emirates, United States and Yemen. *Nationals of Asean countries, France, Laos and Kampuchea* do not require visas for visits not exceeding 1 month. *Nationals of Afghanistan, Iran, Iraq, Libya and Syria* do not require visas for visits not exceeding 2 weeks. *Nationals of Bulgaria, Rumania and the Commonwealth of Independent States* (CIS) do not require visas for visits not exceeding 1 week.

Note: The concessions mentioned above are solely for the purposes of tourism and business only. All visitors must also have entry facilities to a destination beyond Malaysia and must be in possession of a confirmed air ticket to do so. For any further stay or purpose of employment, a visa will be required. *Visa applications* should be made well in advance at the nearest Malaysian diplomatic mission or, in countries where there are no Malaysian representatives, to the British Consular Representative. *Visitors wishing to extend their stay* (on arrival) may apply at the Immigration Office in Lebuh Pantai, two days before the visa expires. It is an offence to overstay the validity of the visit passes - therefore read carefully the visit passes endorsed on your documents.

Health Requirements   Smallpox and Yellow Fever vaccinations are not required for travellers entering Malaysia, except for those who have visited endemic zones 14 days (for smallpox) or 6 days (for yellow fever) prior to arriving in the country. Children are exempted from this ruling, for yellow fever if they are under 12 months old, and, for smallpox if they are under 6 months old.

Customs Information   Items such as cameras, watches, pens, lighters, cosmetics, perfume and portable cassette players are duty free in Malaysia. Visitors bringing in dutiable goods such as video equipment may have to pay a deposit of up to 50% of the value for temporary importation, refundable when they leave. You are advised to carry the receipt of purchase. If you pay any tax or deposit, please ensure that you are given a receipt.

> **Trafficking in illegal drugs in Malaysia carries a mandatory death penalty**

Business & Banking   Shops generally open from 9.30am to 7pm while supermarkets and department stores operate from 10am to 10pm daily. *Banking hours* are from 10am to 3pm on weekdays and 9.30am to 11.30am on Saturdays. The main banking district is Lebuh Pantai, with several establishments at Komtar and its surrounding commercial district.

Currency & Credit Cards   Ringgit Malaysia is the official legal tender. Notes are in RM5, RM10, RM20, RM50, RM100 and RM1000 denominations ~ coins in 1-cent, 5-cent, 10-cent, 20-cent, 50-cent & RM1. Travellers cheques may be cashed at commercial banks and authorised money changers, and are accepted in leading hotels, restaurants & department stores. Major international credit cards such as American Express, Diners, Mastercard and VISA are accepted in leading hotels, restaurants and shopping complexes.

Moneychangers   Licensed money changers operate in Lebuh Pantai and Jln Mesjid Kapitan Keling. They provide a convenient means of exchanging foreign currency as they operate from 8.30am to 6pm. Rates are usually displayed on a board and are often better than the bank rates.

Communications

Cables/Telex   May be sent through Telegraph Offices located at the following :
1 Bangunan Tuanku Syed Putra, Lebuh Downing
   Tel 261 0791 (24 hours)
2 Bayan Lepas International Airport
   Tel 643 9494 (8.30am-9.30pm)

Telephone Services   Calls within Penang made from public telephone booths costs 10 cents and can be dialed direct. Calls to other parts of Malaysia can be made from public telephone booths with subscriber Trunk Dialing and charges will be according to tariffs. Half rates for interstate calls apply after 6pm. For international calls, dial 108 for the operator.

Postal Services   Most hotels provide postal services. There are Post Offices throughout the State. The General Post Office in Lebuh Downing opens from 8am to 6pm daily except on Sundays and public holidays. Letters of up to 20gm sent within Malaysia and Singapore cost 30 cents. For other countries around the world, please inquire at the nearest Post Office for the current airmail rates.

Useful Telephone Numbers

Customs Department	262 2300
Ferry Service	331 5780

General Hospital	229 3333
General Post Office	261 1555
Government Information Centre	261 6677
Immigration Department	261 5413
Penang Development Corp	643 2111
Penang International Airport	643 4411
Penang Port Commission	261 2211
Penang Tourist Centre	261 6663
Tourist Information Centre	261 4461
Tourism Malaysia	262 0066
Tourist Police	261 5522

Railway

Penang (Booking Office)	261 0290
Butterworth (Station)	331 2796
Penang Hill Railway	828 3263

Telephone Assistance & Emergencies

Local Operator	102
Directory Enquiries	103
Telegram Service	104
International Operator	108
Police & Ambulance	999
Fire Brigade	994

What to wear   Light casual clothes recom-mended for travelling. Informal clothes are generally acceptable. **Remember** - no shorts or bare shoulders when entering mosques.

Etiquette & Customs   Shaking hands is the customary form of greeting for both men and women. Remove your shoes when entering a Malay home or mosque, or a Chinese or Hindu temple.

Tipping   Hotels and restaurants add a 10% service charge plus 5% Government tax (from Jan 1 1986); no futher tipping is necessary.

Taxis   Taxis do not use meters - agree on the price before boarding. Note if taking taxis from the airport - daily rates double after midnight!

Trishaws   3-wheeled vehicles run on pedal-power. Found in the vicinity of Georgetown, the minimum rate per mile is RM3 - agree on the price before boarding.

Buses   Stops at designated stands through-out the state. Air-conditioned buses are also available. Main interchange terminal at Komtar (near Ground floor of Yaohan Department Store). Also opposite Jln Penang entrance of Komtar, in front of the temple. Another is outside ferry terminal in Weld Quay.

Travel Notes

Local Bus Company Numbers

- Kenderaan Juara (covers town)   261 0478
- Yellow Bus (to island's south east)   262 9357
- Lim Seng Seng (Air Itam)   262 4212
- KGN Hin Bus Co (North Coast)   890 5094
- Sri Negara   261 1597

Vehicle Rental Renting cars or motorbikes allow you to travel at leisure. Asean passport holders can drive with a valid driving licence from their country of origin. All others must possess a valid international licence. Bicycles are also available for rent. Vehicles drive on the left side of the road. Seat belts are compulsory (crash helmets for bikes). Speed limit - 80kmph; town - 50kmph.

Local Fruits Penang is famous for its tropical fruits which may be eaten or even taken as a juice at most coffee shops, hawker stalls and restaurants. Some of these fruits are rambutans, jambu, guavas, watermelons, mangoes, chiku, mangosteens, starfruit, jackfruit, langsat, soursop, papaya and honeydew. Furthermore, there is a fruit known as the durian. Be forewarned, the combination of its unique smell, taste and texture is an acquired taste.

Language

Although English is still widely used in Penang, the national language of Malaysia is Malay. Formally introduced as the medium of instruction in all national-type schools in the late 60's, it is a relatively simple language to learn and use.

The words provided below are grouped to allow for simple communication when used in their given order. It may not be perfectly grammatical when used in this fashion, but you should be understood.

Pronounciation of Malay vowel sounds are, roughly, "ah" (for "a"), "er" as in "brother", or, "eh" as in "pet" (for "e"), a short "ee" as in "pit" (for "i"), "or" as in "oar", or, "oh" as in "boat" (for "o"), and "oo" as in "put" (for "u"). For pronounciation of double vowel sounds, each is pronounced separately, as in "maafkan", ("mah" and "ahf") and "semua" ("oo" and "ah").

Pronounciation of consonant sounds differ only for the the letters "c" ("ch" as in "chair"), and "sy" ("sh" as in "shoe").

Greetings

good morning	selamat pagi
good afternoon	selamat petang
good night	selamat malam
good-bye	selamat tinggal
good journey	selamat jalan

Courtesies

excuse me	maafkan saya
thank you	terima kasih
you are welcome	sama-sama

Interrogatives

who	siapa
where	di-mana
when	bila
why	mengapa
what	apa
how	bagaimana

Pronouns

I / me / my / mine	saya
you / your / yours	kamu
he / she / his / her / hers	dia
they / them / their / theirs	mereka
this	ini
that	itu

Adverbs

back	balik
carefully	berhati-hati
now	sekarang
quickly	cepat-cepat
soon	akan
today	hari ini
tomorrow	besok
yesterday	kelmarin

Verbs

arrive	tiba
buy	beli
can	boleh
do	buat
drink	minum
eat	makan
enter	masuk
exit	keluar
find	cari
get	dapat
go	pergi
have	ada
help	tolong
laugh	gelak ketawa
leave	lepas
like	suka
lose/lost (something)	hilang
see	tengok
sell	jual
show (indicate)	tunjok
sleep	tidur
sit	dudok

Verbs

stand	berdiri
understand	faham
want	mahu

a negative is indicated by placing the word "ta'" or "tidak" (which means "no"), or, "jangan" (which means "do not"), before the verb.

Nouns

afternoon / evening	petang
airplane	kapal terbang
airport	lapangan terbang
article / goods / item	barang
banana	pisang
bay	teluk
beach	pantai
beef	daging lembu
boat	bot
book	buku
boy	budak lelaki
bus	bas
cape	tanjung
cat	kucing
chicken	ayam
child	kanak
chillie	cili
cigarette	rokok
clothes	pakaian
coffee	kopi
crab	ketam
cruise ship	kapal pelancungan
daughter	anak perempuan
dog	anjing
ear	telinga
eye	mata
face	muka
father	bapa
feet	kaki
fingers	jari
fly	lalat
food	makanan
friend	kawan
girl	budak perempuan
hair	rambut
hairdresser	penyolek rambut
hand	tangan
head	kepala
hill	bukit
hotel	rumah rehat
husband	suami
island	pulau
magazine	majallah
man	lelaki

Nouns (cont'd)

milk	susu
moneychanger	penukar wang
monkey	monyet
morning	pagi
mosquito`	nyamuk
mother	emak
mountain	gunung
mouth	mulut
night	malam
noon	tengah hari
nose	hidung
police station	balai polis
post office	pejabat pos
prawn	udang
price	harga
railway station	stesyen keretapi
restaurant	restoran
river	sungai
sea	laut
ship	kapal
shoe	kasut
shop	kedai
shopping centre	pusat membeli-belah
son	anak lelaki
stomache	purut
sugar	gula
taxi	teksi
tea	teh
teeth	gigi
time	waktu
toilet	bilik air / tandas
tourism	pelancungan
train	keretapi
trishaw	beca
wife	isteri
woman	wanita
younger / older brother	adik lelaki / abang
younger / older sister	adik perempuan / kakak

the plural form in Malay is just a repitition of the noun word eg. "kasut-kasut" for "shoes", "rokok-rokok" for "cigarettes".

Adjectives

a little	sedikit
a lot	banyak
all	semua
bad	burok
big	besar
black	hitam
blue	biru
cheap	murah
chinese	cina

Travel Notes

Adjectives (cont'd)

empty	kosong
expensive	mahal
female	perempuan
full	penuh
full (as in "not hungry")	kenyang
good	bagus
hungry	lapar
indian	india
less	kurang
male	laki-laki
malay	melayu
more	lebih
pretty	cantik
red	merah
small	kecil
salty	masin
sour	masam
sweet	manis
thirsty	haus
white	putih
yellow	kuning

Directions

behind	belakang
front	hadapan
go down	turun
go up	naik
here	di sini
left	kiri
right	kanan
slow down	kurang laju
stop	berhenti
there	di sana
turn	belok

Road Names and Descriptions

drive	persiaran
highway / expressway	lebuhraya
junction	simpang
lane	lorong
road	jalan
street	lebuh

Numbers

quarter	suku
half	setengah
three-quarters	tiga suku
percentage	peratus
one	satu
two	dua
three	tiga

Numbers (cont'd)

four	empat
five	lima
six	enam
seven	tujoh
eight	lapan
nine	sembilan
ten	sepuloh
eleven	sebelas
twelve	dua belas
twenty	dua puloh
twenty-one	dua puloh satu
one hundred	seratus
one thousand	seribu

Time

Time is expressed by the word "pukul" (which literally means "hit"), or "jam" (the word for "hour")

followed by the time (given as a number), and -

qualified by a period in the day, as to whether the hour is for the morning ("pagi"), afternoon and evening ("petang"), or night (malam)

eg. 01:30 AM ("pukul satu setengah pagi")
01:15 PM ("pukul satu suku petang")
10:00 PM ("pukul sepuloh malam").

01:30 AM ("jam satu setengah pagi")
01:15 PM ("jam satu suku petang")
10:00 PM ("jam sepuloh malam")

Personal Notes

Personal Notes